INVADERS AND
THE ROMANS
A MASTER FILE

Compiled by
D C Perkins, BA (Hons), MEd, PhD (Wales) and E J Perkins, BSc (Hons), MEd
Illustrations by Anthony James

MASTER FILES are planned for use in the classroom. Each consists of teachers' notes, pupils' resource material, worksheets, ideas for project work and assessment tables. Each book covers part of the National Curriculum in depth allowing the teacher to decide the amount of material to use according to the age and ability of the pupils.

All rights reserved. This book is not copyright free. It is sold subject to the condition that it shall not, by way of trade or otherwise, be lent, hired out or otherwise circulated without the publisher's written consent. No part of this publication may be reproduced, stored in a retrieval system, or transmitted, in any form or by any means, electronic, mechanical, photocopying, recording or otherwise without the prior written permission of the publisher. All pages in this book can be photocopied for educational purposes only within the purchasing school or educational establishment. There is no limit to the number of copies that may be produced within the purchasing school or establishment and no return in respect of any photocopying licence is needed. This permission does not extend to the making of copies (e.g. in a resource centre) for use outside the institution in which they are made, nor to the making of copies for hire or re-sale.

DOMINO BOOKS (WALES) LTD
SWANSEA SA1 1 FN
Tel. 01792 459378   Fax. 01792 466337
email: sales@dominobooks.co.uk
www.dominobooks.co.uk
The Romans Master File © E J P & D C P 1994 10th printing 2006 (revised and updated)
ISBN 9781 85772 070 9 or (ISBN 1 85772 070 9)

CONTENTS

This book is planned to introduce pupils to the early history of Britain. It forms part of the National Curriculum for Invaders and Settlers, KS2 - the Celts, Romans, Anglo-Saxons and Vikings. Also in this series: Castles, Victorians, Second World War. We also have a wide range of educational activity packs on historical themes.

INTRODUCTION
TO THIS NEW UP-DATED EDITION

During Key Stage 2, pupils learn about important people, events and places from both the recent and the distant past. They learn about change and continuity in their own area, in Britain and other parts of the world. They look at history in a variety of ways, for example from political, economic, technological, scientific, social, religious, cultural and aesthetic perspectives. They use different sources of information to help them investigate the past both in depth and overview, using dates and historical vocabulary to describe events, people and developments. They also learn that the past can be represented and interpreted in different ways.

THE NATIONAL CURRICULUM

A 'sense of history' is an important consideration and teachers should bear this in mind. This book is in three main parts:

   I. Teachers' Notes and Resources concentrating on important Roman themes.
   II. Visiting Historical Sites.
   III. Pupils' Worksheets.

The National Curriculum in history lists major categories of material. These include primary sources and interpretations of sources (books, computer software, films and drawings).
   Useful sources for the study of the Romans include:

DOCUMENTS AND PRINTED SOURCES
Mainly secondary material - see booklist

ARTEFACTS
Clothes
Tools
Furnishings
Household goods
Weapons
Materials concerned with death and burial
Materials concerned with religion

PICTURES
Films
Television programmes about the Romans

BUILDINGS AND SITES
Villages
Farmsteads
Fortifications

COMPUTER-BASED MATERIALS
Software concerned with early times

THE ROMANS

MATHEMATICS
Logistics of the extent
of the Empire
Time-chart
Roman coinage
Army pay
At the market
Rising prices

ENGLISH
Roman vocabulary
Latin and English
Cloze tests
Sequencing
Letter writing
Imaginative writing
A Roman list
Writing and speeches
Word searches
Word puzzles

SCIENCE
Analysis of Roman remains
Architecture
Building techniques
Engineering techniques
Hypocausts
War strategies
Natural resources and uses
Animal husbandry
Food and its storage
Road technology
Use of materials

THE ROMANS CROSS-CURRICULAR LINKS AND ACTIVITIES

ART
Roman design
Fashion
Decorations
Mosaics
Roman jewellery
Roman art

GEOGRAPHY
Map work
Roman army sites
A Roman census
Towns and villas
Hadrian's wall
The Antonine wall
Roman farming,
distribution
and techniques

RELIGION
Death
Burial
Superstition
Sacrifices
Soothsayers
Temples
Ceremonies
Life after death
The State
Religion
Local gods
Festivals
The coming of
Christianity

LAW
The legal system
Jurisprudence
Crimes
Punishments
The legacy of Rome
The legal status of
Romans and slaves

SOCIOLOGY
Emperors
Roman society
Slaves
The position of
the army in Roman
society

TEACHERS' NOTES AND RESOURCES

HOW TO USE YOUR MASTER FILE

For many experienced teachers these few lines will seem superfluous. This book is planned to introduce pupils to the history of Britain. The degree of difficulty varies throughout the book. Following the National Curriculum guidelines, it is especially helpful for those between 7 - 11 years but there is much to interest younger children at the beginning of their study of British history and it provides a background for older children as they proceed to more advanced work.

1. All the material in this book is photocopiable as defined on the title page. This means that all the material can be used in any way you wish in the classroom situation. Drawings may be photocopied and adapted for further work.

2. Covering sections of the master copies with plain paper enables resource material to be used in different ways. The questions may, if you wish, be omitted and you can use the drawings with your own questions.

3. Reduction of the A4 master copies to A5 means that they can be stuck in children's exercise books. The master copies can also be enlarged to A3 to make it easier for students to work on them as a group.

4. Some of your photocopies can be cut up to make additional puzzles and games.

5. It is intended that material be used at different levels depending on the ages and abilities of your pupils.

6. It may be possible to use some of the Teachers' Notes directly with more advanced and brighter students.

7. Some of the worksheets and resources are more difficult than others and the teacher decides the selection of appropriate material.

8. Some of the copy in the teachers' resources may be used in other ways, e.g. as cloze tests, sequencing exercises and so on.

9. Much of the completed work may be used as visual aids around the classroom.

10. Project work may be done individually, in groups and/or with teacher participation.

We hope you enjoy using this book and welcome any comments.

CHRONOLOGY OF EVENTS

Briefly introduce pupils to Rome and show them on a map or a globe where it is. Emphasise that their history started from small beginnings and Rome grew from a Republic (explain this) into a mighty Empire led by a supreme Emperor. Point out the importance of good leaders in the context of Rome (and for that matter any country). Illustrate this by reference to the four great emperors of the 2nd. century - **Trajan** (98 - 117AD), **Hadrian** (117 - 138AD), **Antoninus** (138 - 161AD) and **Marcus Aurelius** (161 - 180AD).

Point out that Roman history covers a long period of time. For two thousand years they dominated history and the ancient world for 500 years - it began in 753 BC and lasted until 476 AD in the West and 1453 in the East (Byzantium). Establish this long history in the minds of your pupils by working out a simple time - line (see below). This can be added to as studies proceed and can be used as a basis for a wall chart.

Remember to say that the British invasion and settlement was only a small part of Roman history. The fact that they could conquer lands far from Rome is significant.

A ROMAN TIME-LINE

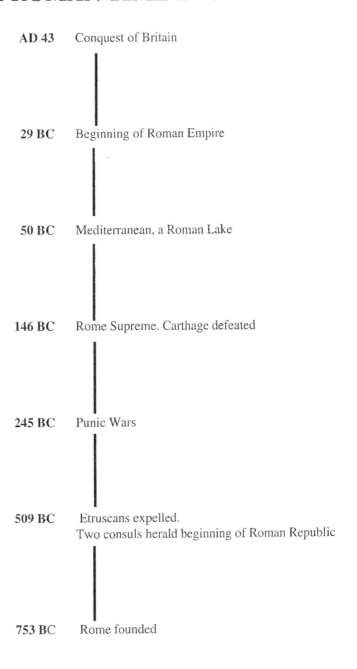

AD 43	Conquest of Britain
29 BC	Beginning of Roman Empire
50 BC	Mediterranean, a Roman Lake
146 BC	Rome Supreme. Carthage defeated
245 BC	Punic Wars
509 BC	Etruscans expelled. Two consuls herald beginning of Roman Republic
753 BC	Rome founded

LEARNING ABOUT THE PAST

Children need to know how historians find out about earlier times: Rome and the Romans, their triumphs and eventual failure. We build up a knowledge of the past from a variety of sources and the picture is continually changing as additional evidence unfolds, more research is undertaken and new techniques such as carbon dating enable us to make more accurate deductions. The evidence comes from the following.

1. **ARCHAEOLOGY** Many Roman sites in Britain have been investigated. Objects from Roman times found include utensils, military equipment and pottery. Animal bones and plant remains give information about Roman diet. There are still many sites not fully examined.

2. **AERIAL PHOTOGRAPHY**

3. **RADIOACTIVE CARBON DATING**

4. **THE REMAINS OF ROMAN BUILDINGS** such as palaces, baths, mosaics, houses, villas, amphitheatres and hypocausts. Remember Pompeii and what happened there. Sculpted gravestones give us clues to the history of individuals.

5. **BURIAL SITES**

6. **THE REMAINS OF ROMAN SYSTEMS AND WATER COURSES** - e. g. aqueducts.

7. **SCULPTURE AND WORKS OF ART** many of which still remain. Note that a prime source for details of the Roman army is **Trajan's** column erected in Rome in AD 113. Its sculpted frieze gives an account of the Emperor Trajan's successful military action against the Dacians (Romania today). It highlights the full range of army activities - in sieges, battles, building camps, marching, felling trees and seeking provisions. Remember to mention mosaic pavements.

8. **OBJECTS USED BY THE ROMANS** which survive such as coins, household wares, bric à brac.

9. **THE WRITINGS OF THEIR HISTORIANS AND OTHERS Tacitus** is a typical example. But remember that many of these writers were interested in literary style more than anything else. Also, many recorded past events may have been biassed or inaccurate. **Vegetius,** for example, described the structure of the legions but he wrote a century after they had disappeared and misunderstood some of the ancient records he used. Occasionally, documents giving accounts of the lives of ordinary people have been preserved on wooden tablets and papyrus.

10. **ROMAN LEGAL DOCUMENTS** Remember that Roman Law is still an important part of most legal systems today including British law. Students still study Roman jurisprudence.

11. **LANGUAGE** Note the importance of Latin historically and today.

12. **DOCUMENTS** and other printed sources.

ROMAN NAVY AND ARMY

The Roman navy and army were crucial to the conquests and settlements of other lands so it is important to consider their history and composition. Children are usually interested in the development of fighting forces and should find lessons on both the navy and army interesting. Drawings of the galleons and the way Roman soldiers were dressed are good points of discussion. There are also plenty of opportunities for role play. Children can find out about the life of the Roman fighting man. They can compare what it was like then with life today. (Remember there are women in the forces now.)

It is important to show what Britain was like before the Roman invasion, what the Romans found here and the effect of the invasion on the Celts.

SHIPS AND SAILORS

Unlike other nations, (e.g. Greeks and Phoenicians), the Romans had no naval traditions. However, after the **First Punic War** (264 - 261 BC) they developed naval power and capability. Using Carthaginian warships as a model, the Romans soon had 200 ships. Warships were essential if they were to reach other lands.

There is little information about these vessels because no wrecks have been located. We do know that the first warships were called **quinqueremes.** Some historians suggest that these were rowing vessels which had five banks of oars. Others say that this would not have been practical and suggest instead each ore was pulled by five men.

A later development was the **trireme.** This fighting vessel had three banks of oars pulled by slaves below deck. A trireme was more manageable than a quinquereme because it was lighter, narrower and more manoeuverable. It also had a single large sail so that it could make use of the wind.

The trireme carried a type of drawbridge wih a spike on the end. This was called the **corvus** and while the ship was not in action, it was stowed against the mast. When an enemy vessel was alongside, the spike was lowered into the enemy's deck and held the ship securely so that the Roman soldiers could board it using the corvus as a kind of gangplank. They then engaged in hand-to-hand combat. Other warships were equipped with rams which were used to make holes in the enemy's ships below the waterline.

Roman warships were slow, cumbersome vessels. Their speed was about 19 km (12 miles) per hour. More than anything, the warships were troop carrying vessels (very much like the Spanish Armada of Elizabethan times), rather than fighting vessels: the soldiers did the fighting while the ships were stationary.

It was the development of an efficient navy that allowed Rome to sail and conquer other lands. They came to Britain across the sea.

A TRIREME
(The Byzantine empire took the best of Roman and Greek ideas about warships and built the 'Dramon'. These were large vessels with three masts and two banks of rowers. They were fitted with catapults and war engines.)

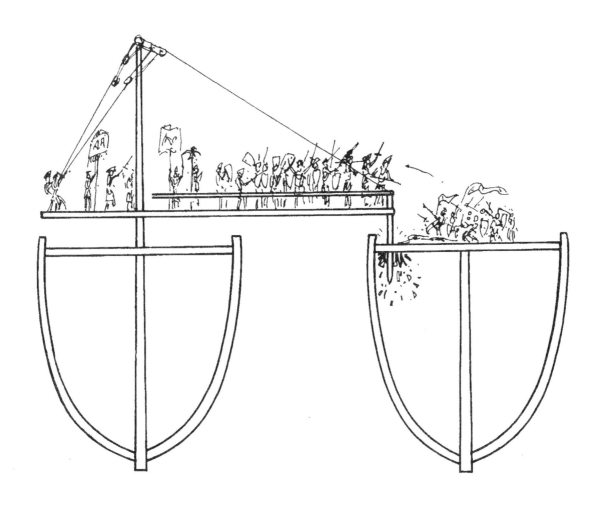

A CORVUS AND DRAWBRDIGE

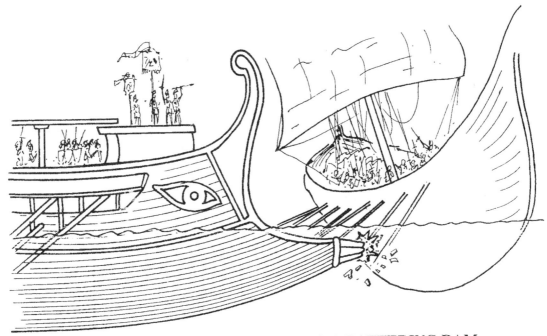

A ROMAN WARSHIP FITTED WITH A BATTERING RAM

THE ROMAN ARMY

In early days, Rome was defended by part-time soldiers who were mainly farmers. They were unpaid and summoned in times of emergency to fight for their country. As soon as the emergency was over, they returned to their farms. By about 340 BC wages were paid to encourage men to join the army and the Republic could raise nearly 800,000 men. Part-timers were phased out and men were recruited who wanted to make military life their career. In a crisis all male citizens between 17 and 46 years of age were obliged to join the army.

In these early Republican days soldiers were grouped into legions of about 4,200. There were different 'grades' of soldier and distinctions between rich and poor were related to the positions they took up in battle. By 100 BC the Republican army had been reorganised by **Commander Marius.** The changes included:

1. All citizens were allowed to join including those who did not own property.
2. Wages were raised.
3. Encouragement was given to full-time recruits.
4. Everybody was given the same training and weapons.
5. Most soldiers were infantry (foot-soldiers).
6. There was a small cavalry element.

These changes were adopted throughout the Empire.

ORGANISATIONAL CHANGES

1. **The Legion.** This was still the main unit and consisted of about 5,000 men (varied between 4,800 -5,000). The Roman army had between 27 - 30 legions. The officer commanding a legion was called the **legate** or **legatus legionis.** He was usually from a wealthy family. Each legion had an eagle made of silver called an **aquila** which was symbolic of the legion's power. It was carried in battle by a soldier called an **aquilifer.**

2. **The Cohort.** This was the main tactical unit. There were ten cohorts in a legion. One cohort called the **prima cohors** had 800 men and was larger than the other nine which had 480 men in each. Each cohort was led by a junior officer called a **tribunus militum.**

3. **The Century.** There were six centuries (units of 80 or 100 soldiers) in a cohort. Each century was commanded by a **centurion** and his second-in-command was called an **optio.** Each century also had a **tesserarius,** a commander of the guard. A standard bearer called a **signifier** carried the emblem of the century and also had other duties.

4. **The Contubernium.** This was a group of eight soldiers who shared a tent and ate together. There were ten contubernia in one century. Each soldier belonged to a contubernium.

5. **Auxilia.** These were non-citizens who supported a legion. Mainly from the provinces, they were organised into cohorts of 500 or 1000 men. They were not so highly trained as legionaries and were paid less. However, at the end of their military service, they were granted Roman citizenship.

THE CHAIN OF COMMAND

LEGION
(Consisted of 10 cohorts. Numbers varied between 4,800 and 5,000 men.
There were approximately 30 legions in the Roman Army.)

↑

COHORT
(Consisted of 6 centuries. About 600 soldiers in all.)

↑

CENTURY
(Consisted of 10 sections of 8 - 10 men. This was the essential fighting unit.)

↑

CONTUBERNIUM
(The basic unit of 8 men (legionaries)who shared a room at barracks and a tent when on campaign.)

Officers included **(a) the Legatus Legiones** who commanded a legion,
(b) the Primus Pilus who commanded a cohort and
(c) the Centurion who commanded a century.

CLOTHES, ARMOUR AND WEAPONS

Equipment (especially armour) might be different even for soldiers in the same unit.

LEGIONARY

Clothes in peace
1. A linen undershirt.
2. A simple, short-sleeved, knee-length woollen tunic worn over the undershirt.
3. Open-work boots (**caligae**) cut from a single piece of leather. They were laced high up on the shin and had thick soles covered with hobnails.

Clothes for war
1. A helmet (**galea**) made of iron or brass. Hinged metal cheek pieces laced together protected the face.
2. Flexible segmental armour called the **lorica segmentata.** This was made of overlapping segments of thin iron sheets linked internally by leather straps. It weighed about 10 kg and folded like a concertina for storage.
3. Bare legs were protected by a large and heavy rectangular shield called a **scutum**. This was curved to fit the shape of the body. (The shield was made of thin sheets of wood glued together and encased in leather or linen and reinforced by metal bindings.)

Weapons
A legionary's personal weapons were two javelins, a sword and a dagger.
1. The **javelin (pilum)** was used in battle but not for individual combat. It was skilfully fashioned so that it bent on impact and could not be thrown back by the enemy. As the ranks of the legion closed on the enemy, two volleys of javelins were thrown to kill and maim as many as possible. Then with swords at the ready, the legion advanced for close combat.
2. The **gladius** or **sword** was worn high on the right side of the body. It was short and two edged (50 cm long) and was drawn underarm with the right arm. The scabbard made of wood bound in leather and with brass trim was attached by four rings to a narrow shoulder belt.
3. A legionary also had a broad, buckled waist-belt called a **cingulum.** The dagger or pugio hung on his left hand side. The dagger was used if he lost his sword or to 'finish off' an opponent.

CENTURION
A centurion had
1. a leather arming doublet.
2. a shirt of mail or scale armour.
3. a cloak of fine material.
4. highly decorated shin guards - silver plated.
5. a highly decorated belt - silver plated.
6. a helmet with a transverse crest .
7. **a sword worn on the left - opposite way to a legionary.**
8. a dagger worn on the right - opposite way to a legionary.
9. a vine stick which was carried as a badge of rank.
10. If a centurion was decorated for valour, he might wear a set of silvered medals (**phalerae**) over his shirt of mail.

In cold climates, soldiers were permitted to wear leather breeches (similar to woollen trousers) called **brachae.**

Children enjoy pretending to be Roman soldiers. Get them to close their eyes and imagine that they are a legionary or centurion. They can imagine the long route marches and setting up camp. They can practise marching, and giving and taking orders. In groups, they can make cardboard armour covered with metal foil using template models of Roman body armour and helmet. They can also make sandals and shields. Some may prefer to wear togas like ordinary citizens. Encourage photography: photographs of the children usually look very realistic. Standard bearers, auxiliaries and cavalry all had distinctive dress which children can research for themselves.

A ROMAN LEGIONARY'S UNIFORM

HELMET (Cassis or Galea)
made of hammered bronze or iron.
It had a sloping neck guard and
hinged, protective cheek guards.
Plumes were worn on ceremonial
occasions.

THICK SCARF (Focale)
to stop the armour chafing
the skin around the neck.

BELT (Cingulum Militare)
A badge denoting rank
was worn here at all times.

LEATHER APRON
This had protective
metal discs.

SWORD (Gladius)
A short 60 cm weapon
used for thrusting at
close quarters.
A legionary wore this
on the right side.

MILITARY SANDALS
(Caligae)
made of leather with thick
soles with iron hob-nail
studs. In winter woollen
or fur 'socks' were also
worn.

JAVELIN (Pilum)
A two metre long throwing
weapon which pinned down
the enemy. It bent on contact
with the enemy so that it could
not be thrown back.

SHORT-SLEEVED
LEATHER OR WOOLLEN
TUNIC (Tunica)
which reached to the the middle
of the thigh.

BODY ARMOUR
(Lorica Segmentata)
of wrought iron designed to
protect the chest and shoulders.
It was formed from overlapping
metal strips held together with
leather strapping, buckles and
hooks.

DAGGER (Pugio)
An iron dagger which
was doubled edged.
It was used in battle
if the legionary lost his
sword. It was also useful as
a general cutting tool.

ITEMS NOT SHOWN
BREECHES (Bracae)
Knee length trousers worn in cold
weather.
WOOLLEN CLOAK (Sagum)
used in cold weather.
SHIELD (Scutum)
This was made of layers of wood,
linen and leather and was curved
to fit around the body. It had a
metal boss in the middle. It was
used defensively to protect the
legionary's body and offensively to
push the enemy off balance.

A ROMAN'S CENTURION'S UNIFORM

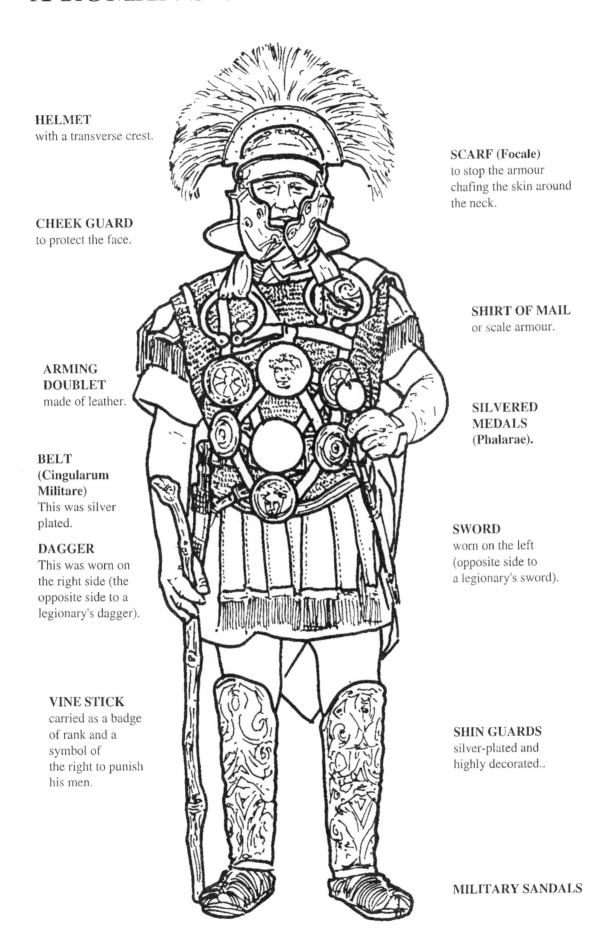

HELMET
with a transverse crest.

CHEEK GUARD
to protect the face.

**ARMING
DOUBLET**
made of leather.

**BELT
(Cingularum
Militare)**
This was silver
plated.

DAGGER
This was worn on
the right side (the
opposite side to a
legionary's dagger).

VINE STICK
carried as a badge
of rank and a
symbol of
the right to punish
his men.

SCARF (Focale)
to stop the armour
chafing the skin around
the neck.

SHIRT OF MAIL
or scale armour.

**SILVERED
MEDALS
(Phalarae).**

SWORD
worn on the left
(opposite side to
a legionary's sword).

SHIN GUARDS
silver-plated and
highly decorated..

MILITARY SANDALS

ROMANS IN BATTLE

THE LIFE OF A ROMAN SOLDIER

By 100 BC most soldiers of Rome were full-time professionals. When a Roman citizen joined the army he took an oath of allegiance to serve the emperor well. The succecss of the army was based on training, on discipline and careful, thorough planning.

The training was hard and vigorous. Each day there were two periods of military drill. All soldiers had to learn to swim. Running, jumping, javelin-throwing and fencing were all part of the régime. Much depended on troops moving quickly to troubled areas and so route marches were arranged three times a month. These were long usually over a distance of 30 km or 18 miles long.

Legionaries were trained to set up camps which were well organised and planned precisely and carefully. These were always laid out in the same way so that everyone knew where everything was. First, the camp was laid out in a square. Secondly, the commander's headquarters were placed at the centre of the camp. Thirdly, the inside of the square was divided into rows and the tents pitched along these rows. They were pitched some distance from the perimeter so that they could not easily be fired upon. Fourthly, a trench was dug around the outside of the camp. The soil from this was made into a mound and a wooden palisade erected on it. Fifthly, lookout towers and defensive weapons were placed at intervals along the palisade.

When the terrain was difficult, soldiers had to carry much of their equipment. This included all their weapons and belongings, food, tools for digging and building, cooking materials and two heavy wooden stakes for the camp palisade. As well as learning armed combat, some soldiers were trained as surveyors, engineers and stonemasons. These were responsible for the construction of permanent forts, roads, canals and other buildings.

Discipline was harsh and if soldiers misbehaved they were flogged. Any disobedience resulted in rations being cut. If mutiny was suspected every tenth man was executed - the word for this was **decimatio.**

Legionaries were quite well paid. They had 225 denarii annually under **Caesar** and this increased to 300 under **Domitian** (AD 51 - 96). Out of this they had to buy their own food which cost about 100 denarii. Professional soldiers served for 20 years, later extended to 25. They were then discharged and given a 'golden handshake' - a lump sum of money or a small plot of land.

LEGIONARY'S STANDARD EQUIPMENT

This is some of the kit carried by a legionary on the move.

TWO STAKES (**Pila Muralia**)
Made of wood with handgrips in the centre, they were used to make a palisade.

COOKING POT

GRID IRON
COOKING EQUIPMENT
(**Instrumenta Culinaria**)

MESS TIN

LEATHER SATCHEL (**Culleus**)
This was tied to a wooden pole and carried over the left shoulder. It contained spare clothes, sandals, a leather water bottle, rope, pans and rations for a fortnight.

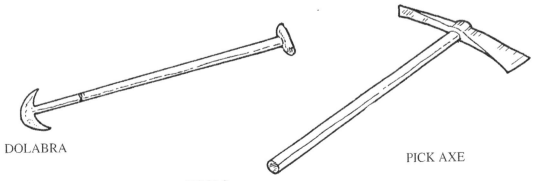

DOLABRA

PICK AXE

TOOLS

Tools carried included a dolabra, pick axe, sickle, saw, a chain, a rope and a net bag.

BRITAIN AND THE ROMANS

In 55 BC a force of ten thousand Roman soldiers commanded by Julius Caesar landed in Kent. The cavalry who formed part of the invasion fleet were prevented from joining the main force, the infantry, by the weather and the tides. The waiting Celtic tribesmen were no match for the Romans but they fought hard and forced the invaders to withdraw. Many of Caesar's ships had been wrecked or beached and he sailed for France after carrying out the necessary repairs.

A year later in 54 BC Caesar again attacked Britain. He did not underestimate the fighting ability and courage of the Celts. He had spent a year in preparation and had hand-picked soldiers from five legions. He sailed from Boulogne in perfect weather and landed in Britain unopposed. While at anchor some of his ships were damaged by unfavourable winds but this time he did not retreat and marched to Wheathampstead, the hill-fort of **Cassivellaunus,** one of the most powerful of the Celtic kings. After a savage engagement the Britons sued for peace and Caesar demanded regular payments to the Empire and took a number of hostages back to Rome.

The real conquest of Britain began almost a century later. In AD 43 an army sent by **Emperor Claudius** landed in Richborough. The general in command of this large contingent was **Aulus Plautius.** It was an opportune time to invade. The Belgic warlords had become very aggressive and were hated by their neighbouring Celtic tribes. The most important of them was **Cunobelinus** (Shakespeare's Cymbeline), the chief of the **Catuvellauni** in Hertfordshire and the **Trinovantes** in Essex. He had set up a major trading centre at **Camulodunum** (Colchester) and was the most powerful king in southern England. Cunobelinus died, however, and his riches were coveted by an exiled prince named **Bericus**. He appealed to Claudius for help in restoring some of this wealth which had been taken from him by the aged king. The Romans responded hoping that they could share in the spoils.

The two sons of Cunobelinus (**Togodumnus** and **Caractacus**) would have none of this and decided to oppose the might of Rome. Togodumnus died in one of the first engagements but Caractacus fought on bravely. He withstood the Roman onslaught at the battle of the River Medway for two days. He was eventually defeated and fled to Wales where for eight years he organised opposition to Roman rule. Finally, he was captured and his family taken in chains to Rome. His proud bearing and bravery impressed Emperor Claudius who spared his life and he lived out the rest of his days in honourable captivity in Rome.

Two independent territories in southern England which had taken no part in the battles now submitted to the Romans. The first was known as **Regni** ruled by a king named **Cogidubnus** from his capital of **Noviomagus** (Chichester). This king was so helpful and co-operstive that Claudius gave him more land and conferred on him the title of King snd Legate to the Emperor in Britain. Later, Cogidubnus became a Roman citizen and took the name of **Tiberius Claudius Cogidubnus.** He was so well thought of that he was able to build himself a splendid Roman palace at **Fishbourne,** where he lived until he died at the age of 80.

The other tribe who wished for peaceful co-existence with the Romans was the Iceni of East Anglia. When their king **Prasutagus** died in AD 60 he named Emperor Nero co-heir of his land and wealth with his widow and daughters. By now, however, the Romans felt stronger and they ignored the dead king's wishes, plundered his kingdom and household, raped his daughters and flogged his widow.

The Iceni led by **Boudicca** (or **Boadicea**) and her daughters rose against the oppressors as a result of this iniquitous treatment. They took Camulodunum, ousted the retired legionaries living there, massacred the small community and its inadequate garrison and then marched on **Londinium** (London). After laying Londinium waste, Boudicca laid siege to **Verulamium** (St. Albans). In all 70,000 people are estimated to have died in these three towns.

Suetonius Paulinus, Governor of Britain at this time was away dealing with the Druid community in Anglesey when the revolt started. He hurried back and engaged the rebel enemy at Fenny Stratford in Buckinghamshire. Boudicca drove her chariot with its axles sprouted with knife blades, urging her warriors to defeat the Romans. *Win the battle or perish . . . That is what I, a woman, intend to do. Let the men live in slavery if they wish.* These brave words of Boudicca were reported by the Roman historian, Tacitus. But the trained legionaries with a large cavalry element were too strong for the now over-confident Celts. The defeated Boudicca is said to have fled.

The **Brigantes** in the Pennines and the **Silures** in southern Wales were later problems for the Romans. Between AD 71 and 74 the Brigantes were systematically defeated and then the Silures and Ordovices in central and northern Wales. **Agricola** who became governor of Britain in AD 78 built a network of forts and roads in the Pennines to keep the Celtic tribes subdued and in AD 80 began to advance into Scotland. Building forts to subdue the natives as he went, his campaign reached its zenith in AD 83 when he fought and destroyed the combined armies of Scotland at the **Battle of Mons Graupins.** In AD 84 before he could complete his work he was recalled to Rome.

The Picts in Scotland were also troublesome and made forays into Roman territory for a number of years. During a visit to Britain in AD 121 or 122, the **Emperor Hadrian** ordered the building of a barrier ten feet thick.

across the country between what is now Wallsend-on-Tyne and Bowness-on-Solway. This wall had a castle every mile, and 16 bigger forts with larger garrisons at irregular intervals. Later, further north another wall called the **Antonine Wall** was built between the Forth and the Clyde (AD 142).

Within Britain the Romans adapted buildings and built new ones. Their cities were constructed on a grid plan and linked by straight roads. In garrisons and administrative centres they established shops, temples, barracks, amphitheatres, potteries, glassworks, mints, bath houses and villas. **Eburacum** (York) became an important military capital. Chester **(Deva)** became a legion headquarters from AD 70 and **Caerleon** an important military headquarters in Wales. **Aquae Sulis** (Bath) became known in the Roman world for its warm springs and London became established as a trading centre.

By the fourth century Britain had become Romanised. Successful officials and collaborators with the Romans built villas and taught their sons Latin. Barbarians from eastern Europe now began to attack Britain as elsewhere and the Picts and Scots renewed their attacks from Scotland. The Irish attacked Wales in the north west. The only way Rome could defend Britain was by paying imported mercenaries. The Angles, Saxons and Jutes added their weight to the other invaders. Roman Britain was at an end.

Children should know what tribes existed in Britain when the Romans invaded. (See our National Curriculum book on the Celts.) They should be able to analyse the strengths and weaknesses of the Romans and understand how Britain was conquered by them. Again, role play may be important with one group of children being the Romans and another being the Celts. Children might enact a simple play with the main characters of Boudicca and Caractacus. Simple mathematical problems on the organisation of the Roman army and the life of a Roman soldier could be set. The construction of a model Roman camp shows how effectively it was planned. What were the strengths of this planning? Were there any weaknesses? How would the soldiers have coped if the terrain or other reasons had made it impossible to carry out the instructions precisely?

Consider the Roman invasions from the Celtic point of view. Consider how the Romans could deal with the Celts. When and why did the crisis become overwhelming for the Romans?

Consider with the children how the Romans tried to contain opposition to them. The Hadrian and Antonine Walls are important here. Would such structures be relevant today? The children can read about these for themselves. Discuss the use and value of Roman roads in dealing with problems in Britain. Are the children surprised that the roads were straight and that Roman towns were built on a grid system?

Also consider the view that the Romans never really conquered the Britons but merely placated some of them while some worked with the Romans (quizlings?) and many carried on a guerilla warfare against the imperialists until they left.

Most tribes were eventually subdued but there was never a time when the whole island was subject to Roman rule. Consider this last statement in the light of modern history - the French resistance against the Germans, the IRA and the British, the Spanish and the Basques.

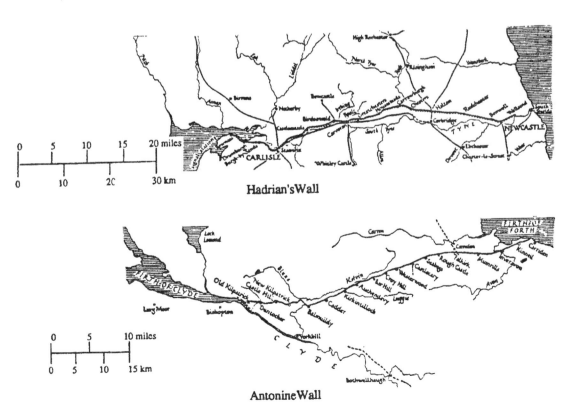

0   5   10   15   20 miles

0   10   2C   30 km

Hadrian's Wall

0   5   10 miles

0   5   10   15 km

Antonine Wall

THE ROMANS IN WALES

The Romans had to deal with a great deal of resistance to their invasion and rule from those in Wales. The four main Celtic tribes were thorns in Roman flesh. These tribes were

The Silures - in modern Gwent and Glamorgan,

The Demetae - to the west of the Silures and in modern Dyfed,

The Ordovices - in central Wales and the north west,

The Deceangli - in modern Clwyd.

Most resistance came from the Silures and Ordovices. However, Caractacus (or Caradog as he was known in Wales) having been defeated by the Romans in the east fled to Wales and for almost eight years organised opposition to Roman rule in terrain that was ideal for guerilla warfare. To help subdue Caractacus and the Silures the Romans built a strong fort at **Glevum** (modern Gloucester). Caradog was determined to keep Roman forces out of Wales for as long as possible and he moved his sphere of interest from the Silures to the Ordovices of Powys and planned a pitched battle with the enemy. In 51 AD, choosing a site which gave him greatest advantage (steep hills and overhanging cliffs, an easily defended river with no fords or easy crossing places) he engaged the enemy. From Caradog's point of view, the battle was a complete failure. The Britons were out-manoeuvred and out-fought, ejected from their chosen position and temporary fortifications by the superior skill and equipment of the Roman troops led by their general **Ostorius Scapula.** Caradog escaped but his family was taken. Seeking refuge in the palace of **Queen Cartimandua** of the Brigantes, he was betrayed, put in chains by her and delivered to the Romans.

The Romans did not or could not deal with the problems they encountered in Wales as a whole. Instead, they dealt with them piecemeal, responding to each problem as it arose. The next military problem concerned the Island of Mona, Anglesey (Ynys Mon today). Resistance to Rome from there was organised by a large community of Druids who were fanatically antagonistic to Rome. The governor in 59 AD was Suetonius Paulinus. He had been a seasoned campaigner in Africa where he had defeated the tribes of the Atlas Mountains. Paulinus was not only keen to wipe out the material resistance the Druids provided but he also wanted to destroy the native cult associated with these priests. The attack was carefully planned. The Romans used landing-craft suited to the shallows of the Menai Strait. There was a moment of hesitation when the legion was terrified by the sight of the enemy backed by praying and cursing priests accompanied by wild women devotees waving flaming torches. However, the Roman battle-line pressed forward to victory. Anglesey was garrisoned and the sacred groves systematically destroyed.

The next governor, **Iulius Frontinus,** decided to subdue the Silures. He used sea power to occupy the rich and fertile sea-plain of Glamorgan. He believed that once a foothold was won, the conquest of the whole of South Wales would follow.

Once these military conquests had been made, the Romans decided to build forts throughout North and South Wales and on the Welsh borders to subdue and control the Welsh. Legionary fortresses were established at Isca Silurum, Glevum, Viroconium and Deva as well as a number of auxiliary forts and fortlets elsewhere.

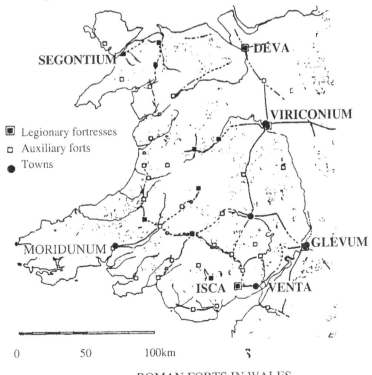

SEGONTIUM

DEVA

VIRICONIUM

■ Legionary fortresses
□ Auxiliary forts
● Towns

MORIDUNUM

GLEVUM

ISCA · VENTA

0   50   100km

ROMAN FORTS IN WALES

THE ROMANS IN WALES

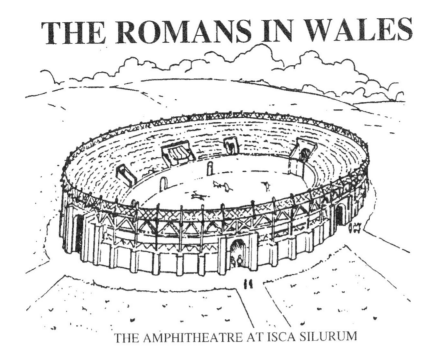

THE AMPHITHEATRE AT ISCA SILURUM

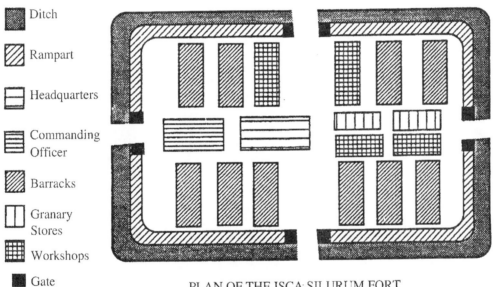

- ▨ Ditch
- ▨ Rampart
- ▤ Headquarters
- ▤ Commanding Officer
- ▨ Barracks
- ▥ Granary Stores
- ▦ Workshops
- ■ Gate

PLAN OF THE ISCA SILURUM FORT

The history of the Romans in Wales is in many senses the history of the Roman army living in forts and much can be seen at places like Isca Silurum (modern Caerleon) where the Second Augustan Legion was based.

The Romans were anxious to get as much from Wales materially as it could provide. Local produce was used by the numerous garrisons throughout the Principality. Lead was mined in Clwyd and West Wales, copper came from Anglesey and silver from North and West Wales.

The lead mines in Flintshire were working by 74 AD. Lead was a very important metal for the Romans because the only way the Romans could produce silver was by cupellation from lead and in the Roman world, silver was the most regular money of account. This explains the rapid development of Welsh (and British) lead resources.

Only one gold mine of the Roman occupation in Britain is known and that was the Welsh mine at Dolaucothi, near Pumpsaint (between Llanio and Llandovery in north east Carmarthenshire). The workings were both open-cast and long and deep adits (cave-like mines) but it is not known how much gold was extracted.

Finally, there is one further reminder of Roman habitation in Wales. This is the small Roman villa which has been located at Llantwit Major in South Glamorgan. This estate developed in the second century AD and was administered from a simple courtyard house with small farm-buildings attached. This small villa provides a contrast with the large, palatial buildings of **Fishbourne** and elsewhere. John Storrie excavated the site in 1888 and discovered that the main house was deserted and had fallen into ruin in the fourth century AD. However, the barn-dwellings continued to function as an economic unit for another 100 years. Many skeletons were found on the site and this Roman villa is shrouded in mystery.

FORTIFICATIONS AND DEFENCE IN ROMAN TIMES

The Romans had one of the best armies in the world and became very good at defending themselves from their enemies and at launching successful attacks against them.

Hadrian's Wall built between 122 AD and 129 AD to protect the south of Britain from attack from the north stretched for nearly 130 km (80 miles) across the country from the River Tyne to the River Solway. It was over 45 m (15 ft) high and in some places 3 m (10 ft) thick. Built into the structure approximately equal distances apart were 16 large forts. Each of these garrisoned an auxiliary cohort of 1000 men or a cavalry division of 500 men and their mounts. 79 towers were built along the wall at intervals of one Roman mile (1500 m or 5000 ft). These were manned by sentries who acted as lookouts and could send messages to other parts of the wall, There was a parapet on the top of the wall which protected troops as they walked along it. A final defence was a large ditch which was built in front of the wall to deter aggressors.

Besides permanent fortifications, the Romans built ditches and walls around their camps and towns and became adept at attacking forts and castles that stood in their way. The strategy of a Roman siege included the following.

I. They built siege-works which were in reality wooden scaffolds to enable the Romans to climb up the walls of the besieged building.

2. They built siege towers which could be pushed against the walls. Soldiers hid in these and were protected as they got close to the walls.

3. They approached the walls by covering themselves completely with their shields which protected them from enemy fire. This formation was called the testudo, the tortoise.

4. They used numerous other weapons including
   (a) **tormenta** which could hurl stones and missiles over long distances.
   (b) **catapulta** which fired a bolt and was manned by two men (this was also called the scorpio).
   (c) **battering rams,**
   (d) large heavy **catapults, onagers,** which could fire huge rocks and stone over 500 metres (1600 ft).
   (e) large stationary catapults (the **ballista**) were also used to fire smaller missiles or burning debris.

ATTACKING FORMATIONS IN ROMAN TIMES

The Romans practised special military formations which they carried out to the letter in battle situations. In formation, soldiers advanced as a body to break up and then smash enemy lines. Some of the formations were:

1. The wedge Small groups of soldiers pushed through enemy lines. (Still used by police today to break up crowds.)

2. The square If surrounded by an enemy, soldiers formed into this defensive formation. It consisted of interlocking shields with javelins used as pikes at all angles. It was often called the 'prickly hedgehog'.

3. The tortoise (See above, also called the **testudeo.**) Men in close rank covered themselves with shields locked together at the front and over their heads. The body of men could then move forward slowly protected against the missiles hurled at them by the enemy.

THE REASONS FOR THE ROMANS INVADING BRITAIN

The main reasons include the following.

1. The expulsion by Cunobelinus of his son Adminius who appealed for help from Emperor Gaius in AD 40.

2. The Roman view that their empire was superior to all others. Virgil's admonition, *Remember you are a Roman,it will be your job to rule over other countries, so that the world becomes peaceful and everyone obeys the law.*

3. The desire to conquer. Rome wanted to 'dominate' the world.

4. The pride of Emperor Claudius and his need to be famous. Also, to show that he was superior to previous Roman invaders who had failed to take Britain.

5. Roman prestige. It was important to Rome to conquer other countries.

6. Greed. The Romans wanted more and more.

7. To punish Britain for helping Gaul and to ensure such help would not be possible again. This was especially important in Caesar's day.

8. The quest for riches, commodities and produce. These included wool, leather, timber, corn, fruits, oil, glass and wine. Also, metals especially precious ones such as silver and gold as well as tin, iron, lead and copper. The need for slaves.

9. Other requests for Roman help, e.g. the request of Bericus.

10. The need to punish the Belgae, one of the most warlike of the Celtic tribes who had fought bitterly against the Romans in Gaul. Caesar, in particular, wanted to take his revenge on them. The disturbances of the Celts on the Gallic coasts had to be punished.

Consider why Britain was invaded. Surely the country was too small to be worthy of such action? What do you regard as the main reason for invasion? The children may have reasons of their own. Was the invasion worth it? How far did the invasions contribute to the downfall of the Roman Empire? Note Strabo's reasons: *corn, cattle, gold, silver and iron . . . these are brought from Britain: also hides, slaves, and clever hunting dogs.* Remember that in Britain, the principal metal produced was lead and the only way of producing silver known to the ancient world was by cupellation from lead. Silver was essential to the Romans: it was the most regular money of account and they needed vast quantities.

INVADERS OR SETTLERS?

Consider whether the Romans ever intended to 'settle' in Britain.

Discuss the pros and cons of colonisation by a superior power.

Are there good and bad aspects of colonisation? (Consider Rome, France, Germany, Britain and the Soviet Union as colonising powers.)

Whether the Romans intended to stay after using Britain's resources is a moot point.

The children can usefully present information and opinion in two columns headed JUST INVADERS and REAL SETTLERS.

What evidence of real settlement exists?

ROMAN TOWNS IN BRITAIN

Romans were essentially town dwellers. To them towns were a sign of civilisation. It is no wonder that in Britain they took over established townships like the early Celtic settlement **Calleva** (Silchester). They also developed health resorts like **Aquae Amemetiae** (Buxton) and **Aquae Sulis** (Bath). Many of the towns in Britain developed from an earlier military presence such as **Deva** (Chester) and **Isca Silurum** (Caerleon). Roman towns tended to have the following characteristics.

1. Easy access - easily reached by roads and rivers. If the roads did not exist, the Romans built them.

2. Shops, a market place and some industry like glass or pottery making.

3. A forum in the town centre. People could meet and commerce flourished there. A **basilica** (town hall) was the government centre in the town.

4. Walls or ditches to protect the citizens from their enemies.

5. Aqueducts brought clean water to the town. Baths, sewers and drains to keep the townspeople clean and healthy.

6. Entertainment facilities including a theatre and an amphitheatre.

Roman towns were organised on a grid plan (which they had learned from the Greeks). Many had two main streets, one running north to south, the other running east to west. The other streets also ran at right angles to each other leaving square spaces between them. These spaces were called insulae (islands). A town had a number of gates (usually four) giving access to roads to other towns. Roads outside were lined with tombs and graves for burials were not allowed inside a town's walls. At a point where the two main streets crossed stood the forum with a basilica, a large building used for government, for law-giving and public functions.

Important features in Britain included the public baths, the theatre, the amphitheatre, Roman temples and districts including apartment blocks or large houses occupied by wealthier citizens. There may also have been inns **(tabernae)**, snack bars **(thermopolia)** and bakeries **(pistrina).** In some areas there were stepping stones so that citizens could keep their feet dry. There were large drains or gutters so that water could drain away. These also served as sewers for a town's waste. The Romans were skilled engineers and besides their excellent roads they built bridges, arches and water systems. The last-named were essential for towns needing water for public baths and lavatories. Thus, most towns had water flowing into huge cisterns along aqueducts (pipes set into bridges or laid underground). It was then distributed through a complex system of lead or earthenware pipes. Water was also used as a source of power to turn waterwheels. The Romans also developed a heating system for their houses which must have been useful in inclement Britain. This heating was called the hypocaust. When a house was being constructed, fireplaces were put in the basement. The floor at ground level was supported by pillars of concrete or brick. Fires were lit in the grates and the warm air escaped under the floor and through ducts in tbe walls. The floors and pillars retained the heat.

The children should learn to compare Roman towns with present-day British towns. Consider how life for the Romans in towns was different from ours. The Romans had little industry, no mechanised transport - there was no danger of pollution from vehicles in these days. Let the children reflect on how 'modern' the Romans were and how sophisticated their organisations were in contrast to the early Britons. If possible, outline the construction of a typical Roman town and illustrate how 'earlier' towns hampered Roman construction and development. The use of concrete was developed in the second century BC and the Romans also knew how to make mortar out of volcanic ash but still much of the layout of a typical town was of wood - compare with the present-day and also discuss the problems and dangers of fires.

ROMANS IN THE COUNTRYSIDE

In the southern half of Britain, wealthy merchants, landowners and leaders did not like living in the towns. Instead, they built stone villas in the countryside.

Typically, a Roman villa was a large house surrounded by its own extensive lands. Such villas were both country residences and productive farms. The sites of about 500 villas have been found in Britain. A few of the most famous are Chedworth in Gloucestershire, Lockleys near St. Albans, the Rockbourne Roman villa near Fordingbridge in Hampshire and Bignor near Chichester. There was plenty of living room in these houses and even separate quarters for servants and slaves. Animals were housed outside. Central heating and hot water for baths were provided by hypocausts. The walls inside were richly decorated with designs on fine plaster and even the floors were covered with mosaics (mosaic pavements). Roman mosaics were patterns and pictures made of small coloured pieces of stone and brick set into plaster while it was wet. Black and white mosaic patterns were very common designs. A typical Roman villa would have the following.

1. Summer house.

2. Entrance hall.

3. A living room **(atrium)**. This did not have much furniture but might have a pool for bathing in the centre.

4. Dining room **(triclinium).** This would have tables for holding and displaying the food and couches for those eating.

ROMAN LIFE

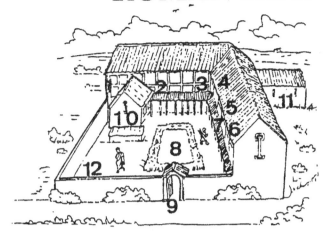

A ROMAN VILLA

5. Kitchen for cooking food. This was done on wood or charcoal stoves.
6. Larders and stores to house produce from the farmland surrounding the villa.
7. A verandah to stroll along which overlooked the courtyard below.
8. Courtyard - a place for a garden with plenty of flowers and an area for growing herbs.
9. Entrance.
10. Slaves' quarters - separate accommodation for those who waited on the family.
11. Bath house - a place where the family could take regular baths and relax.
12. Shrine (lararium) see aside for worshipping Roman gods.

Consider with the children the benefits of living in a Roman villa instead of in the town. Let them imagine they are the owners of a villa and how they would spend their lives. Compare and contrast life in a Roman villa with life in a modem house or flat.

Remember to point out that many Romano-British villas were small. As one historian points out *Comfortable on the average, luxurious at best, and squalid at worst.Romano-British villas ranged in size from cottage to mansion . . .* Also point out that the owners of villas were mainly British and they represented the adoption of Roman standards. If possible take the children to a 'local' villa and let them see it for themselves. The plan of a typical villa is fairly simple. Let them draw a plan and then draw a villa A villa can also be made from *papier-maché* with some help from you or their parents. No consideration of villas is complete without some mention of mosaic pavements. Note some of the most famous and find some pictures if possible such as the **Wolf and Twins pavement** from Aldborough (in Kirstal Museum, Leeds), the **Venus pavement** at Rudston (East Yorkshire), the **Apollo and Marsyas pavement** from Lenthay Green, Sherborne (Dorset). and the **Venus** and **Gladiators, Head of Winter, Medusa** and **Ganymede** and **Eagle mosaics** at Bignor (Chichester).

ROMAN FAMILY LIFE

At the outset Roman family life depended on whether the family lived in the town or country.

In a town, most ordinary people lived in a large apartment block (**insulae**) and only the very wealthy could afford a private dwelling (domus). Some apartments were luxurious but most were cramped. Families may have had a few rooms or one. Insulae could only be built four or five storeys high. Poorer tenants lived at the top of the house which was usually built of wood. Woodburning braziers were the only form of heating and there was a risk of fire. Landlords often built extra rooms on to apartments to make more money: these were often unsafe and liable to collapse. Insulae had no internal drains and people threw their waste into street gutters. Few of them had toilets and people had to use public lavatories. There was no running water and people carried it from public fountains. Some occupants, especially richer tenants, had several, comfortable, well furnished rooms on the second or third floors. Lower storeys were made of stone. Cooking was unusual in such buildings and people had cold meals and went to inns and bars for hot food. Access to the upper storeys was by a staircase. People did not normally live on the ground floor. Rooms at this level were used for trade - shops, inns, bars or taverns were typical.

Private houses were unusual but wealthy Romans and Britons lived in these. They were usually on one level. The rooms at the front opened on to the street and were often rented out for trade. The farnily lived in the rooms at the back of the domus. They ate food in a dining room and received guests in the **atrium.** Most homes had no bathroom because there were so many public baths. Glass windows were rare and wooden shutters or animal skins maintained privacy. In warm climates these were left open. There was often a large,

well equipped kitchen in a domus. Servants (slaves) cooked the food. Most large houses had a walled garden (**peristylium**) and a shrine to the household gods was erected there. Many houses had a sturdy front door with a lock to keep out strangers and thieves. One of the slaves was a door keeper. The Romans developed their own heating system (**the hypocaust**).

Continue the work on towns: in particular, a typical Roman town and how it was organised. Show the children how it was planned and the important features. Consider with them life in an apartment block and in a domus. Compare and contrast life in Roman towns/cities with life today. Help them to research and write accounts (with drawings) of life as it was lived by typical Romans - a slave, a trader, a tenant, a landlord.

In the countryside, poor people lived in simple wooden huts. The rich lived in villas. Compare and contrast town and country life in Roman times. Also compare and contrast their town and country life with life today.

HOW HOUSES WERE FURNISHED

Many rooms were too small for furniture and there were no carpets. Wooden furniture was usual but some was made of marble or metal. The atrium and tablinum were the main family rooms which were furnished. Tables were widely used and these could be low, especially for dining. Beds and couches were important and they were used not only in bedrooms but also in dining rooms and studies. The Romans had a variety of chairs, stools and even folding chairs. The cathedra was a high curved chair usually used by old people. Heavy chests and cupboards were made for storage. Romans used oil lamps, lanterns and tapers to light their houses and small bronze braziers for heating: they burnt mainly wood, charcoal or coke. There was no wall paper but walls inside were decorated with paintings and the rich had mosaics laid on the floors.

FOOD AND EATING

Most small houses and flats had no kitchen and hot food was obtained outside in bars and taverns. Richer people had large, well equipped kitchens staffed by slaves. Food was cooked in earthenware or bronze pots on a stove. Charcoal was used in these. Meat and poultry were roasted on spits over fires. Sharp knives were used to chop vegetables and a pestle and mortar used to grind herbs and spices and similar ingredients. Wine or oil was stored in two-handled pots called **amphorae.** The Romans had a variety of pots, jugs, pans and strainers.

The main meal of the day was called the **cena.** This was taken in late afternoon after a visit to the baths. Other meals included breakfast and lunch **(the prandium).**

TYPICAL MEALS

Breakfast - bread, wheat biscuits, honey, figs, dates or olives, water or wine.
Prandium (lunch) - bread, leftovers from the cena the night before, walnuts, figs and dates.
Cena - the main meal of the day. (During the republic this was very simple consisting of wheat - porridge, vegetables and sauces.) In Britain, this had become quite lavish. There were a number of courses and fish and a variety of meats were eaten.

A ROMAN FEAST

In rich households the main meal of the day became a lavish affair. It was a time to entertain friends and guests and hosts showed their wealth by giving sumptuous meals. In early times only men could attend formal dinners but in imperial times women joined them. At formal feasts there was a correct seating order. (Surely to be expected. Today we still have 'top table' at formal functions.)

At formal feasts or banquets each couch seated three people. The couches were called **summus, medius** and **imus** (top, middle and bottom), and diners were seated according to their social status. The most honoured guests sat at medius 3, and the host often sat next to him at imus 1. A very rich host might have two tables of nine people each. Less formal dinners often had fewer.

Note that a central table held the food and the family and guests sat around it on couches on three sides. The fourth side was left clear for slaves to bring food and remove empty dishes. Romans did not use knives or forks. They ate with their fingers and sometimes with spears. Slaves wiped the guests' hands between courses.

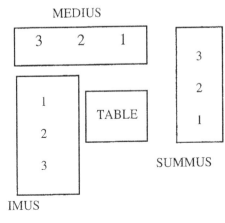

THE SEATING PLAN

There were usually three courses.

First Course Appetisers - salads, mushrooms, oysters, other shellfish and fish. This was followed by a drink called **mulsum** which was wine sweetened with honey.

Second Course A main course of about seven different dishes including fish, game, poultry and meat served with sauces and vegetables.

Third Course Instead of cleaning the dishes after the second course, the slaves removed the table and replaced it with another one. Thus, this part of the meal was called the second tables **(secundae mensae).** Fruit, nuts and honey cakes were served.

Food was brought on serving dishes made of pottery and glass and a variety of wines were drunk from goblets made of the same materials. Wine was available throughout the meals.

Consider Roman meals with the children and compare and contrast the menus with those of today. Also point out the formalised dining and how and when Romans ate. Consider the shortage of hot, cooked food for the poorer classes and the lavish food for the wealthy. Tea and coffee were not available. Why was this? Why did the Romans drink wine? Outline some Roman recipes and say how food was prepared and eaten. If possible plan a Roman meal and a banquet and allow the children to prepare simple Roman recipes. Use cloze texts to reinforce the work and do matching words with meanings to improve Roman vocabulary. Consider the ways of life of those living in poor and in rich households. These could include 'My work as a . . .' slave, waiter, cook, musician, wine-waiter and so on.

CLOTHES AND JEWELLERY

Most people wore clothes made from wool or hair. (In Rome itself, cotton was imported from India in imperial times but was very expensive.) Fur, felt and leather were also used extensively. Professor L. A. Richmond affirms, *The consumption of hides . . . must have been enormous. The Roman army itself used leather for jerkins and breeches . . . shield coverings . . . and tents, not to mention their massive boots.*

Most clothes were made from large pieces of cloth folded and pinned with safety pins **(fibulae)** or belts. Clothes were mainly natural in colour. A man's only underclothes was a loin cloth of wool or hair with a tunic on top tied with a belt. Outdoors, people wore cloaks and trousers. Originally, only Roman citizens wore the garment called the **toga**. This was worn over the tunic. At first it was a large woollen-type blanket but linen was used in warmer climates. Togas were mainly white but senators in Rome wore them with a purple stripe. There were other colours and black was used for funerals. Women wore a loin cloth and sometimes brassieres and corsets as underwear. Over this they wore a tunic and on top a **stola** (a dress which reached the ankles). In early days women wore the toga but later the **palla** became fashionable. This was a large rectangular piece of cloth draped over the stola. Some wore this palla over their heads, others wore a veil or scarf to protect their hair.

Most boys and girls wore the same clothes as the adults, mainly tunics. Young boys might wear the **toga praetesta** which had a purple stripe. Children took part in a special ceremony at the age of 14 and could then wear adult clothes. During the Republic many Roman men had beards but later these became unfashionable and most men were clean-shaven. In imperial times, women favoured curled and plaited hair and some wore wigs of human hair. Women wore make-up and as it was fashionable to be pale, they whitened their arms and faces with powdered chalk. Eyelids were darkened with ash and antimony, lips reddened with red wine or dye from the fucus plant.

Often, the Romans wore no shoes, especially indoors. Outside shoes and sandals were made of leather. Soldiers wore sandals or boots studded with hobnails.

By the time of the Empire, jewellery was fashionable. It was made from gold, silver, bronze, and iron and these were set with precious and semi-precious stones. Opals, emeralds, sapphires and pearls were popular but they sometimes used polished glass instead. Both men and women wore rings and women earrings, necklaces, anklets, hairpins and brooches. In Britain, pearls and amethysts were popular and jet associated with Whitby was used for rings and bangles. Jet came to be endowed with almost magical properties. Hair pins, spindles, pendants and medallions were elaborately carved. Finally, miniature carvings in semi-precious stones known as cameos became very popular.

This section can be used for role play. The children can dress up as Romans and they can make and wear Roman headresses and togas. Consider with the girls the make-up used by Roman women and compare it with the more sophisticated make-up of today. The puberty ceremony at 14 is also an interesting study. Are there any similar customs in Britain today? Consider Jewish ceremonies in this connection. Look at Roman jewellery and allow children to handle it at a local museum if possible. Consider the use of jet and the superstitions associated with wearing it. Discuss hair-styles and fashion in Roman times. Compare and contrast with today.

MARRIAGE, CHILDBIRTH AND BURIAL

Parents chose husbands and wives for their offspring who had no say in the matter. Marriages were arranged for political, business, financial or social reasons. Girls could marry at 12 but usually waited until they were 14. There were different types of arrangements. In early days, a woman's money and goods could become the property of her husband's father. Later, a woman. could retain her own belongings. The wedding day had to be chosen carefully because many days were thought unlucky. The second half of June was believed to be a lucky period and was popular for weddings. .

STAGES IN A ROMAN WEDDING

1.. **The Engagement** A party was held and the marriage contract written out. The bride was given a ring for the third finger of her left hand. The night before the wedding she gave her toys to the gods at the household shrine.
2. **The Wedding Day** The Wife's house was decorated with flowers and ribbons. At the ceremony she wore a white tunic, a head dress of flowers, a red veil and shoes. Her hair was braided.
3. **The Priest** asked the gods if the day was lucky. If it was, the wedding continued. If it was not, the wedding was postponed.
4. **The Contract** This was signed and the chief bridesmaid joined the girl's hand with her husband's. The couple prayed and the bride promised to follow her husband.
5. **The Procession** After the marriage ceremony a party was held at the house of the bride's father then the bride and groom led a procession to the groom's house. The groom then carried his wife over the threshold.

CHILDBIRTH

Childbirth was dangerous in Roman times. Women married early as they believed childbirth was safer when they were young. The newborn baby was bathed and placed at the feet of the father. When he picked up the baby, it was a sign that the baby had been formally accepted into the family. On the ninth day, the child was named and given a charm to ward off evil spirits **(a bulla).** When a boy was 14 and had finished his education, there was a ceremony to proclaim his adulthood. At this, he discarded the clothes of his childhood, was given an adult's toga, had his first shave and was registered as a citizen. Then there was a celebration party.

FUNERALS AND BURIALS

When someone important died, the Romans undertook rituals based on their beliefs. Most Romans believed a corpse was rowed across a river (the **Styx**) to the underworld **(Hades).** The spirit was then examined and sent to heaven **(Elysium)** or hell **(Tartarus).** The funeral prepared the corpse for the journey. A coin was placed under the tongue to pay the fare for the ferry to Hades.

When a nobleman died his body was washed and embalmed with oil. If he had held an official position he was dressed in his robes, if not he was dressed in a toga. The body was then placed in the atrium surrounded by lamps and candles and covered with flowers and wreaths. Relatives and friends came to pay their respects. The corpse was then carried on a litter by 8 men to the funeral. Professional mourners **(praeficae)** and torchbearers followed. The procession was accompanied by music. A speech praising the dead man was given at the forum. The corpse was then taken to a grave outside the town and placed in a stone or marble coffin called a **sarcophagus.** The Romans also believed in cremation. The body was burned in a pit or on a pyre. Food and clothes were thrown into the flames in case the deceased needed them in the afterlife. When the fire had died down, wine was thrown on it. The ashes were collected and put in a jar or urn which was stored in a special chamber **(a columbarium).** The site of a grave was often marked by a stone or monument.

Consider the Roman form of marriage, birth and death with the children. What do they think of arranged marriages? What are the advantages and disadvantages? If there are Muslims in the class, what are their views? The Roman marriage was essentially pragmatic not religious. Consider the pros and cons of marriages with no religious element. Talk about superstition surrounding the event in Roman times. Are there any superstitions about weddings today?
Compare Roman weddings with today's ceremonies. What similarities are there? Pinpoint the differences. Why do people marry?
Why was June popular in Roman times? Why do so many marriages in Britain take place in March?
Consider birth and death in Roman times. Depending on the age of the children, discuss the effects of the fall in the number of people getting married today. What are the reasons for this change?

EDUCATION, JOBS AND OCCUPATIONS

EDUCATION

Children in Roman times were educated according to the wealth and status of their parents. Many poor children received no education at all and started work when they were very young. Those from wealthier families started school at 5 or 6 years of age going first to a primary school (**ludus**). At about 11 years, some boys then transferred to a secondary school (**grammaticus**) There, they were taught history, geography, geometry, philosophy, music and astronomy. There was special emphasis on Greek: the Romans were greatly influenced by the Greeks and much of their culture stems from this nation. Also, many books were written in Greek and children had to read Greek and Roman literature. Girls usually left school at 11 and were taught at home in preparation for marriage. Some boys too, were educated at home by a personal tutor. After secondary school, boys who wanted to become government officials or politicians studied with a **rhetor,** an expert in public speaking. He taught boys from 13 - 14 upwards how to write speeches and how to deliver them. Very wealthy parents might send their sons to Athens or Rhodes to be taught by expert Greek teachers.

In Britain, schools for the children of army commanders and the rich were organised in a similar way because the Romans wanted their colonies to follow the Roman tradition. A slave called a **paedagogus** was employed to take them to school and supervise them. They were often taught by slaves. Most schools consisted of one room and catered for 12 or fewer children at a time.

Pupils learnt much by rote and their memories were reinforced by reading and writing. Because paper was not available, pupils wrote on panels of wood coated with wax, on broken pottery or on material from Egypt called papyrus. To write on wood and pottery, pupils used a pointed metal pen called a stylus. They wrote on papyrus with a reed pen with ink made of gum and soot. The Romans were fond of reading and built up collections of scrolls copied by scribes who were often from Greece. In the 4th. century scrolls were replaced by the codex in which pages could be secured. This was something like a modern book and was easier to carry.

JOBS AND OCCUPATIONS

Wealthy Romans regarded physical work with contempt and would only consider careers in politics, the army or in finance. Skilled work such as planning buildings and treating the sick was undertaken by educated middle-class men, foreigners or freed slaves. Poorer people worked as craftsmen, shopkeepers or farmers but all manual labour was done by slaves. Rich women seldom worked but directed the household, organised the slaves and cared for the children.

SLAVERY AND SLAVES

These people had no rights or status in society and were treated as commodities: they could be bought and sold. As the Roman empire expanded so the number of slaves increased. Slaves did all the menial jobs, the majority were employed in manual work such as building or mining. The cleverest worked in wealthy homes as doctors, tutors, musicians and artists while others worked in administration and on farms. Discontented slaves often rebelled against the Romans. The most famous rebellion was led by the slave, Spartacus, who gathered an army of 90,000 compatriots in 73 BC and fought against the Romans for two years.

MONEY, TRADE AND BANKING

At first, Romans traded by barter that is they exchanged one kind of goods or service for another. As the Roman Empire grew, coins were minted and used to buy goods. The emperors eventually took charge of coin-making, especially the valuable gold and silver ones. Some of the most important coins were

Coin	Made of	Weight
Aureus	gold	8 g (quarter oz)
Denarius	silver	4 g (one-eighth oz)
Sestertius	bronze	
As	copper	
Semi	bronze	
Quadrans	copper	

Later, a gold coin called a Solidus and weighing 5 g (one-sixth oz) was issued by Emperor Constantine.

RELATIVE VALUES

1 aureus was worth 25 denarii.
1 denarius was worth 4 sestertii.
1 sestertius was worth 2 asses.
1 as was worth 2 semis.
1 aureus = 25 denarius = 100 sestertii = 200 asses = 400 semis.

The Romans developed a banking system. The bankers and money lenders, **equites,** as they were called, often worked privately although some were controlled by government. As Rome grew taxes were raised on individuals. Property tax was levied on houses, farms, slaves and animals. Also, tax was levied on inherited money and property and on financial deals. Inflation was high and people did not always have confidence in the coinage preferring to barter.

ENTERTAINMENT, SPORTS AND PASTIMES, RACES, GAMES AND GLADIATORS

The Romans were keen on all sorts of diversions and entertainment. Many of these activities were promoted and paid for by the government. There were three types of entertainment, theatrical events, chariot races and gladiator duels and beast events. The most popular were chariot races and gladiator events especially in Rome where the former drew huge crowds. As many as 24 races could take place in a day with up to twelve chariots taking part. The races were usually started by the emperor and ran over seven laps. There were usually four different teams classified by the colours red, green, blue and white. A central structure called the **spina** stood in the centre of the track and the chariots rode around it. (It was very much like a motor car race today.) Usually two or four horses pulled each chariot and champion charioteers were very popular and became wealthy.

Amphitheatres were built throughout the Roman Empire. These were designed for gladiators and animals to fight in. Gladiators were mainly convicted prisoners, criminals and slaves although some volunteered for the work. Wealthy citizens had the best view and sat near the front: less well off spectators sat high up and further back. Bears, panthers and bulls were encouraged to fight each other. Wild animals were often let loose with defenceless prisoners in the arena. Gladiators fought in the afternoon and a bout usually continued until one was killed. Defeated or badly wounded gladiators could ask for mercy. A thumbs down signal from the emperor meant death and a thumbs up signal meant that the man's life was spared. A successful gladiator could become rich and gain his freedom but this was rare.

Romans were also fond of the theatre and the first stone theatre was built by **Emperor Pompey** (106 - 48 BC). Theatre goers liked comedies and plays by Plautus and Terence were the most popular. Other entertainment included walking in public gardens and parks, running, javelin throwing and wrestling. People also played a game similar to draughts, gambling games like heads and tails (**capita et navia**) and the equivalent of dice (**tali**).

ROMAN BATHS

Huge baths in which many people spent a lot of time together were built in Rome and throughout the Empire. They were built where the water was thought to be healthy. Nero, Emperor of Rome (AD 54 - 68) is believed to have said, *Sanitas per aquas* - health through water. The Romans developed the art of bathing to perfection and public baths or 'thermae' were to be found in every quarter of a Roman city. Bathing was considered to be a pleasure to indulge in and essential for health and vitality. Bathing was an activity which took place in the afternoon and in the early evening as a prelude to a night's entertainment. It was enjoyed by every social class except slaves who were present at the baths only to attend to the needs of the bathers. Men and women bathed separately. People paid a small entrance fee and this covered all the facilities available. A large hypocaust system provided the heat. Bathing involved progression through a series of rooms at different temperatures.

1. The Roman citizen first disrobed in the **apodyterium,** the cloakroom.
2. Then there was the **sudatorium,** a room comparable with today's sauna where a citizen could sit and sweat.
3. The hottest room was the **laconicum.** A tub of boiling water in the centre kept it steamy and the room was used mainly by invalids.
4. The **caldarium** was slightly less hot and bathers splashed themselves with water from the many ornate fountains in this room. It was here that the skin was cleansed using scrapers (**strigils**) and perfumed oils.
5. From the caldarium, the citizen went to cool in the **tepidarium.** This was cooler (luke warm) than the previous baths.
6. Finally, the citizen could dive into the cold bath aptly named the **frigidarium.**

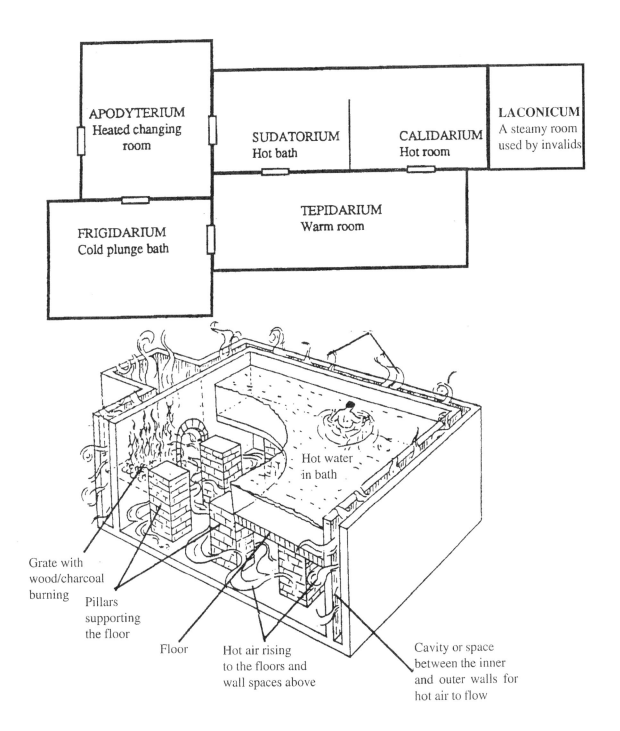

Grate with
wood/charcoal
burning

Pillars
supporting
the floor

Floor

Hot air rising
to the floors and
wall spaces above

Cavity or space
between the inner
and outer walls for
hot air to flow

Hot water
in bath

HYPOCAUSTS

This was a form of underfloor heating. Buildings were constructed with spaces between the inner and outer walls and below the floors. Air was heated by a wood-burning furnace. The hot air rose and circulated throughout the ducts and cavities in the building. Circulating hot air in this way made the buildings very dry and warm. There was also a high risk of fires.

Some baths had libraries, restaurants, gardens, barbers, massage rooms and exercise yards attached. In Britain, there were famous baths at Bath in Somerset and Buxton in Yorkshire. The Romans did not have soap and they removed dirt and perspiration by using oil and scraping it off with strigils (scrapers made of wood, bone or metal).

Romans used a variety of perfumes and extracts. Floral and spiced oils such as jasmine and sandalwood were used to cleanse and perfume the body and hair. Salts were considered a beneficial addition to the waters. Lavender, believed to have been brought to England by the Romans was widely used - *Lavanadum* means fit for washing. Baths were often built where the water was thought to have medicinal properties. People went to them hoping to have their illnesses cured.

Pupils should be given an account of the Roman way of bathing and, if possible, a visit to Bath in Somerset or a similar complex of Roman baths will help them understand the importance and extent of this activity.

RELIGIOUS BELIEFS, GODS AND GODDESSES, SUPERSITITIONS AND FESTIVALS

The Romans believed in many gods and goddesses. Some were worshipped at home and some were worshipped in public.

HOUSEHOLD GODS

The worship of household spirits was the earliest type of Roman religion. They believed their homes were protected by a number of spirits (**numina**). One group looked after the stores (**penates**), the other the entire home (**lares**). Each house had a shrine (**a lararium**). The family prayed at the shrine everyday and offered small tokens or gifts like wine, bread and fruit. Every household had its own protective spirit called the **genius** and spirits from their predecessors called the **manes.** Some numina became gods such as **Janus**, the god of the doorway and **Vesta** goddess of the earth.

PUBLIC GODS

The Greek influence is shown in Roman gods who were worshipped publicly. Most of these Roman deities came from Greek gods. Worship followed strict rituals and ceremonies. The Romans also believed in sacrifices. Each god was considered to have special powers: one looked after matters to do with war, another looked after the underworld and so on. Large temples housed the statues to these gods and priests, government officials, musicians and others processed to the shrines and offered sacrifices on public holidays and festivals.

ROMAN GOD	GREEK NAME	INFLUENCE
Jupiter (most important god)	Zeus	god of thunder and lightning
Dis	Pluto	god of the underworid
Neptune	Poseidon	god of the sea
Vesta	Hestia	goddess of the earth
Ceres	Demeter	goddess of agriculture
Juno	Hera	goddess of women and childbirth
Vulcan	Hephaestus	god of craftsmen and forges
Mars	Ares	god of war
Venus	Aphrodite	goddess of love and beauty
Diana	Artemis	goddess of the moon and hunting
Apollo	Apollo	god of the sun, music, healing and prophesy
Minerva	Athena	goddess of crafts and war
Bacchus	Dionysus	god of wine
Mercury	Hermes	god of trade (Jupiter's messenger)

There were many other gods of less importance such as **Cupid**, another god of love, and **Roma,** the goddess of Rome itself. In Imperial times, the Emperor himself became a god and was worshipped.

When the Romans conquered other lands they found different religions and gods. Some they discarded, others they adopted. One of the most important of these was Christianity which spread rapidly through the Empire. Christians refused to worship idols and the Roman gods and they were hounded and persecuted. Christians often met in secret and the religion was so strong that it flourished in spite of the way they were treated. In AD 313 the Romans agreed to tolerate Christianity and it became the official state religion eighty one years later in AD 394. Roman and Celtic religions blended and as long as the Britons recognised and venerated Roman gods, there was peaceful co-existence.

SUPERSTITIONS

The Romans were very superstitious and many people made a living from telling the future. Some of the most famous were:

Haruspices an order of priests who looked at the innards of sacrificed animals to decide a god's attitude to government work.

Augurs 16 prophets who could foretell the attitudes of the gods from flocks of birds, cloud formations, thunder and lightning.

Sibyl a prophetess living in caves at Cumae who left writings about interpreting the will of the gods.

Astrologers told fortunes from an examination of the stars and the date of a person's birth.

FESTIVALS

The Romans held many religious and other festivals throughout the year. No business took place at these times and they were celebrated by races, games and theatrical shows. Some of the more important are listed below.

FESTIVAL	DATE	EVENTS COMMEMORATED OR CELEBRATED
Compitalia	Early January	Purification of farm or household
Parentalia	13 - 21 February	Ceremonies to honour dead parents
Lupercalia	15 February	Ceremony to bring about fertility
Caristia	22 February	Ceremony to conclude Parentalia
Tubilustrium	23 March	Future success in battle
Ludi Megalenses	4 - 10 April	Honoured Cybele the Great Mother
Ludi Ceriales	12 - 19 April	Honoured Ceres, goddess of corn
Parilia	21 April	Celebration of the birth of Rome
Ludi Florales	28 April - 3 May	Celebration of fertility and Flora, the goddess of flowers
Vestalia	9 June	Honoured Vesta and bakers
Fors Fortuna	24 June	Honoured the goddess, Fortuna
Ludi Apollinares	6 - 13 July	Honoured the god, Apollo
Ludi Romani	5 - 19 September	Honoured the god, Jupiter
Ludi Plebeii	4 - 17 November	Honoured Jupiter
Rites of the Bona Dea	Early December	Honoured Bona Dea, the good goddess who protected women
Saturnalia	17 December	Honoured the god, Saturnalia

The children should know about the Roman attitude to religion, the names of their main gods and the powers the Romans believed these gods to have. Consider superstitions in Roman times and today. Recount stories about Christian martyrs in Rome and the martyrdom of St. Alban in Britain in particular. Show how Christianity would have been misunderstood in Roman times and the concept of one God instead of many gods would have been alien to them. Let the children imagine they are early Christians and they can write stories about how they would evade capture and if captured what might happen to them.

MEDICINE, TECHNOLOGY AND ROAD BUILDING

In medicine, as in other skills, the Romans owed a great deal to the influence of the Greeks. Much of their knowledge of medicine came from Hippocrates, a Greek doctor who lived in the 5th. century BC. Doctors were trained by young men watching others (the same practice continues today). Medical treatment was a combination of science, religion and superstition. Operations were performed without anaesthetics and wine was drunk to dull the pain. Medicines were made from plants, minerals and animals. **Discorides,** an army doctor, researched about 600 herbal medicines and tested some 1000 drugs on soldiers. The wealthiest Romans had personal physicians: the poor depended on charity. There were male and female practitioners. Throughout the Empire there were temples to **Aesculapius,** the god of medicine. People slept in these temples hoping they would be cured while they slept.

TECHNOLOGY AND ROAD BUILDING

The Romans were highly skilled builders who learned and copied a great deal from the Greeks. They used wooden scaffolds to hold and support blocks of stone and used cranes to lift and position heavy objects. They manufactured bricks and they learned to deal with intricate mathematical and technical engineering problems.

As road building was so important in Britain, this will be considered here. At first the roads in Britain were built to join the forts. The route was planned to be straight and direct - the shortest distance between two points (or forts). Roman army surveyors used a wooden instrument called a **groma** which was used like a modern theodolite*.

A Roman road consisted of a number of layers. First, they laid sand or small stones on the soil. Secondly, they used a layer of large stones mixed with lime cement. Thirdly, there was a layer of concrete, gravel, flints or sand with lime. On top of this were blocks of stone in concrete to ensure a smooth surface. Ditches were dug each side of the roads. Finally, the roads were designed to be higher in the middle so that water drained away into the ditches. Every 8 to 15 miles there were post and relay stations. The Roman roads in Britain connected the main forts and towns and gave easy access to the country. They were built to last and we still use some of them today. They are usually recognised because they are so straight. Three of the longest are **Fosse Way, Watling Street** and **Ermine Street.**

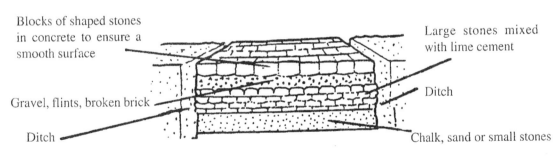

Blocks of shaped stones in concrete to ensure a smooth surface

Large stones mixed with lime cement

Gravel, flints, broken brick

Ditch

Ditch

Chalk, sand or small stones

Cross Section of a Roman Road

This was a device made of wood from which strings with weights were hung (like plumblines). A surveyor could fix a straight line by lining up the path with the strings. If trees or hills got in the way of the line of vision, surveyors lit fires in a straight line and plotted their routes using the smoke.

Consider with the children roads in Britain before the Romans came. How easy would it have been to get around the country? Discuss the importance of roads to the Romans particularly when they were concerned with military matters and controlling the country. What was the importance of roads in communications in Roman times? Could the Romans have controlled Britain without good roads? Why were they so straight? Describe what the roads looked like. Do they exist today? Locate 'old' Roman roads on a map for the children. Help the children to construct a section of a Roman road. Using a plastic tray, put gravel as the base, then coarse sand, then a layer of polyfiller and complete with plasticine stones. Make the road camber so that any water can run off the road into the sides. Why were these roads built in 'layers'? How did water drain away?

Compare with the roads today. Explain why motorways are straight and why most roads are not straight. Discuss the difficulties in building straight roads in modern Britain.

THE ROMAN LEGACY

Elements of Roman civilisation have lasted for centuries and have had a lasting influence on Britain as elsewhere. These are some of the most important.

1. **Without the industry** and perspicacity of the Romans, the knowledge of earlier cultures would have disappeared. Some Greek sculptures and Greek writings exist only in the form of copies made by the Romans.

2. **The Romans** copied and learned from the Greeks. They adapted and extended their knowledge.

3. **The Romans** were urban dwellers and many countries (including Britain) had few towns before they came. Many cities still remain because they were founded by Rome - they chose excellent geographical and economic sites, e.g. London.

4. **The Romans** established travel and communications worldwide. In Britain, their roads were a basis for the modern road system.

5. **Roman architecture and buildings** lasted for centuries. Roman innovation and development - the arch, the dome and the use of concrete - allowed them to build structures which still survive. They perpetuated the architectural skill and styles of ancient Greece.

6. **They gave the world Latin.** Those who were conquered had to learn this language and many European languages - Portuguese, Italian, French, Spanish and Roumanian - are closely linked. The English language still contains thousands of Latin words. Until recent times, official Latin was used by the Catholic church.

7. **Painting and sculpture.** Roman scholarship and the preservation of Greek and Roman literature and statues helped the Renaissance of the 15th. and 16th. centuries. This led to many masterpieces being painted.

8. **Law.** The Roman Legal System is important in world law. Some systems e.g France are based on this entirely and the State of Louisiana in the USA still follows Roman law. Roman law has had a great influence on British law.

9. **Government.** The Roman legacy has inspired governments abroad and the imperialist and republican systems have been tried elsewhere. Other colonial systems have been tried. The EEC may be considered an extension of the Roman system - member states with a common tax system, a ruling organisation and an international court of justice. (The EEC has a common currency.)

10. **Literature and Ideas.** The literature the Romans preserved led to the flourishing of new ideas in later centuries. Their literature is still studied today and much of our knowledge of early times comes from the writings of Roman historians.

VISITING HISTORICAL SITES

THE IMPORTANCE OF VISITS

A visit to a Roman site or a museum brings the threads of the study together. 'Chalk and talk' are now turned into reality. Pupils can see for themselves where the Romans lived and 'seeing is believing'. Observation is the keynote but there may be possibilities of participation in the Roman way of life and of role play. Fortunately, throughout Britain there are many Roman sites and excellent museum displays. Try to visit the chosen site alone before taking a group or class.

PREPARATION FOR A SITE VISIT

BEFORE THE VISIT

Choose a site that is appropriate and can be easily reached or preferably is near to the school. Make a list of the reasons for and the aims of the visit. Decide which National Curriculum topics are to be covered and which attainment targets you wish to meet. If possible visit the site yourself before you take the class. Most sites have teachers' notes and worksheets which are usually helpful and save a great deal of time. You may wish to modify them to suit your class and your own objectives. It is very important to prepare the children for the visit. The site will seem exciting and strange to them when they arrive. They may wander off aimlessly, waste time and possibly get into dangerous situations.

Decide what you are going to tell the children about the site before the visit. Few are likely to be born archaeologists or natural historians and they need enough information to enable them to understand what they will see during the visit. Slides, photographs, ground site plans are helpful beforehand if they are available. It may be useful to talk about Roman sites in general and then discuss the site you are planning to visit in particular. One visit is not going to cover everything and so decide exactly what you want to concentrate on. Depending on the age and abilities of the children, keep it short and keep it simple. Above all, the children should enjoy it educationally and socially.

It may be necessary to enhance the children's visual skills. The visit may involve using the following skills at some level.

1. Observation skills.
2. Recording skills.
3. Being able to make comparisons.
4. Being able to make deductions.
5. Reading, writing and comprehension skills.
6. Measuring skills.
7. Estimating skills.
8. The ability to read maps.
9. The ability to read plans.
10. Mathematical skills.
11. Scientific skills.
12. Social skills, especially sharing and communicating.

A sense of time may be learned from the site and youngsters may realise the importance of historical evidence. Aesthetically, the group may gain a great deal from what they see. Pupils need guidance about the information and data they can gather at the site. Practise for this can be done by organising a survey of the school, school grounds, village or an area of a town before the visit. This should be simple but it is helpful to observe a familiar place closely and discover the relationship between information on a flat piece of paper like a map or diagram drawn by the pupil and the 3D environment.

Devise your own activity pack for use on the site. This should include illustrations, a questionnaire and questions requiring observation and deduction.*

*Domino Books have educational activity packs on the *Romans* and the *Roman Villa*.

TEACHERS' CHECKLIST

On your personal visit before taking your group or class consider the following.

1. **Geography of the land.** Consider this, the lie of the land and the geology of the site.

2. **Location of the site.** Why was the site chosen? Was it a military site or camp? Is it near water resources, a river crossing, or did it become part of a trade route? Did it develop into an important settlement or town?

3. **Previous occupation of the site.** Was the site occupied before the Romans came? If so, how did the Romans change it?

4. **Defence.** Would the site have been easy to defend? Is there any evidence left of defensive structures? Were there multiple points of defence? Is the location ideal for withstanding an attack? Were there any defensive disadvantages? Was the site ever attacked? If so, what was the result?

5. **Attack.** Is it a suitable site from which to wage war? What elements of cover are there for an attacking force? Is the site easy to withdraw to after attacking the enemy?

6. **Weapons.** What has been discovered at the site? What else was probably used?

7. **Discoveries.** Have there been any important discoveries or finds at the site? If so, pinpoint them so that you can discuss them with the children.

8. **When was the settlement used?** Was it used in peacetime or wartime or both?

9. **Buildings.** Consider the buildings. What kinds of homes were they, what was their size and where were they located? Were they mainly for British or Roman occupation or both? Were there any special homes such as a domus or villa?

10. **Size of the community.** Consider the size and social structure of the community. Were there any specialists such as architects, potters, farmers, priests? What evidence is there of slaves and their tasks?

11. **Food.** What evidence is there about diet, cooking and cooking utensils? What can be learned about the storage and preparation of food?

12. **Meat.** Is there any evidence of food processing, meat eating or meat cooking?

13. **Food preservation.** Are there any details of the storage of grain. Was food preserved?

14. **Natural resources.** What were the natural resources of the site - such as wood, stone, clay or charcoal? Were there any natural resources close by? Have these been exhausted?

15. **Skilled work.** Is there any evidence of skilled work such as making cloth, leather goods, weapons, pots and decorative pottery, jewellery ?

16. **Metal working.** Is there any evidence of metal working (lead, tin, bronze, iron, silver, gold) at the site? Look for equipment, tools, jewellery and artefacts.

17. **Other materials**. Is there any evidence of the use of stone, shale, slate or other materials on the site? (If so have they been used practically or aesthetically or both?

18. **Clothes.** Is there any evidence of the production of woollen or linen material and clothes?

19. **Finds of special interest.** Have there been any finds of special interest such as those which conferred status or position - chariot fittings, leather goods, shields, swords, helmets, aquiliae, brooches, mosaic pavements, painted walls?

20. **Religion.** Is there any evidence of religious worship or ceremonies? What gods were worshipped?

21. **Burials.** Is there any evidence of death and burial ceremonies on the site? Were articles buried with the dead? What superstitions existed?

22. **Roman properties.** Is there evidence of items or buildings that are particularly associated with the Romans - hypocausts, baths, strigils and so on?

23. **Decline.** How did the site decline? What came after? How is the site looked after now?

24. **Excavations.** Has the site been fully excavated? What work remains to be done?

SOME SITES TO VISIT

Antonine Wall	Cirencester	Jewry Wall Museum,	Roman Baths, Bath
Bath	City and County	Leicester	Roman Lighthouse,
Bignor Villa,	Museum, Lincoln	Leicester	Dover
W. Sussex	Chichester	Lullingstone,	Roman Villa,
British Museum,	Colchester	Sevenoaks	Rockbourne,
London	Corinium Museum	Lincoln	Fordingbridge,
Burgh Castle,	Cirencester	London	St. Albans
Great Yarmouth	Corstopitum Roman Fort,	Lunt Fort, Baginton	Silchester
Caerleon Museum	Corbridge	near Coventry	Verulamium Museum,
Caerwent	Dover	Maiden Castle,	St Albans
Caister by Norwich	Exeter	Dorset	Verulamium Theatre,
The Castle, Colchester	Fishbourne Roman Villa	Museum of London	St Albans
Chedworth Villa,	near Chichester	Portchester	Vindolanda Roman Fort
Gloucestershire	Fort at Housteads	Rockbourne Villa	Bardon Mill,
Chester	Gloucester	at Salisbury	Northumberland
Chesters Roman Fort,	Hadrian's Wall	Roman Army Museum,	Wroxeter Roman Baths
Chollerford	Housteads, Museum and	Greenhead,	York
Northumberland	Fort, Hexham	Northumberland	

AT THE SITE

Make use of the surroundings of the site as well as buildings there. Let the pupils study their surroundings including flora, fauna, trees (include bark rubbings if appropriate), animal habitats and so on. Instead of or as well as the guidance from activity sheets, the children may be asked to solve a problem from the past. Examples are:

You are commander of this Roman fort. Say how you would prepare for an attack by an enemy.

You are leaving the fort, say what people you would leave behind and why.

Show how this fort was organised in peace time.

A group of foreign tourists who have no previous knowledge of a Roman site is intending to visit the place. List the main features you would tell them about. Why have you chosen these features?

The children may imagine they are Roman citizens at the site. Give them roles to play and work out how these roles may be fulfilled. If it is practical pupils can wear Roman costume and the site can be used to re-enact an event from history such as the revolt of Boudicca, the capture of Caractacus or the rebellion of Sparticus. The use of an unfamiliar site in this way may be difficult and not as useful as using role play as part of the follow up.

FOLLOW UP TO A VISIT

To reinforce the visit you might consider the following when you return to the classroom.

1. Devise a quiz to find out how much the children have learned.
2. Devise other written work especially making them see the site as a place where people lived and worked. How did the site operate on a daily basis? Use actual characters from Roman history if possible.
3. Guide the children to write reports on particular aspects of the site - the Roman barracks in a fort, the forum, basilica and baths in a town and so on.
4. Use the activity pack/worksheets/guide book.
5. Organise the pupils to make a display of any written work - drawings, maps, ground plans, photographs. Develop this for use in the classroom and classify and label any objects. Some children may make models (some accurately scaled) costumed figures and measured drawings.
6. Pinpoint any technology from the site such as roads, buildings or hypocausts. Spinning, dyeing, weaving making weapons or pots are part of this.
7. Pinpoint the diet and ways in which food was cooked.
8. Pupils could make a frieze or collage. Brass or other rubbings may be possible.
9. The pupils could write and act a play or situation which might have occurred on the site such as a conversation between a legionary and centurion about camp life or the attitude of Celts to the Roman occupation.
10. Use slides, drawings, photographs and so on to prepare an audio-visual presentation. Tape-slide sequences or presentations or a video presentation may be possibe depending on the site and the age and abilities of the children.
11. Pupils may examine documents (i.e. copies of documents) from the site. They could ask themselves

When was it written?	How do we know when it was written?
Who wrote it?	Why was it written?

What sort of document is it? (Personal communication, order or command, official or unofficial . . .)
Are there any differences between this document and others? Compare and contrast the documents if more than one is available.

Is it one of a series of documents?	How do we know the original is genuine?

Finally it is necessary to evaluate the visit objectively and write a brief report on how such a visit may be improved next time.

If it is not possible to visit a Roman site, you may be able to get the Romans to visit you'. Contact the Ermine Street Guard. They are a group who recreate the physical appearance of the Roman army. The Guard brings the Roman army alive for visitors to historic sites and museums. It may be possible for them to visit your school. Their address and telephone number are in the book list.

BOOKLIST/RESOURCES

BOOKLIST / RESOURCES GENERAL REFERENCE BOOKS/PUBLICATIONS

Allason-Jones, L.,   *Women in Roman Britain,* British Museum Publications, 1989
Aylett, J. F.,   *In Search of History. Early Times to 1066,* Edward Arnold, 1985
Birley, E.,   *Roman Britain and the Roman Army,* Kendal, 1961
Bishop, M. C. and
Coulston, J. G. N.,   *Roman Military Equipment,* Batsford, 1993
Burn, A. R.,   *The Romans,* Oxford University Press, 1991
Burrell, R.,   *Agricola and Roman Britain,* London, 1953
Collingwood, R. G.,   *Roman Britain,* Oxford, 1924
Collingwood, R. G.,   *The Archaeology of Roman Britain,* London, 1930
Connolly, P.,   *The Roman Army,* Simon Schuster, 1991
Connolly, P.,   *The Legionary,* Oxford University Press, 1988
Connolly, P.,   *The Cavalry Man,* Oxford University Press, 1988
Corbishley, M.,   *What do we know about the Romans?* Simon and Schuster,1991
Grant, M.,   *Romans,* Nelson
and Pottinger, D.,
Haverfield, L. F.,   *The Romanization of Britain,* 4th. Edition, Oxford, 1923
Haverfield, F. and   *The Roman Occupation of Britain,* Oxford 1924
Macdonald, Sir George,
Honnywill, J.,   *The Romans,* Collins Primary History Series, 1991
Johnston, D. E.,   *Roman Villas,* Shire Publications, Aylesbury, 1979
Keppie, L.,   *The Making of the Roman Army,* Batsford, 1984
Pluckrose, H., (ed.)   *The Romans,* Hamish Hamilton, 1981
Renfrew, J.,   *Food and Cooking in Roman Britain,* History and Recipes,
                              English Heritage Historical Building and Monuments Commission for
                              England, 1985

Richmond, L,   *Roman Britain,* London, 1947
Richmond, L. A.,   *Roman Britain,* Penguin Books, 1963
Rivet, A. L F.,   *Town and Country in Roman Britain,* London, 1958
Toynbee, J. M. C.,   *Art in Roman Britain,* London, 1963
Wacher,J.S.,   *The Towns of Roman Britain,* Batsford 1974
Ward, J.,   *Romano-British Buildings and Earthworks,* London, 1911
Watson, G. R.,   *The Roman Soldier,* Thames and Hudson, 1969
Webster,G.,   *The Roman Imperial Army,* A. and C. Black,1985
Wilson, R. J. A.,   *Roman Remains in Britain,* Constable, 1975

                           Life in Roman Times, London Museum Catalogue, No. 3, 1946
                           Rome and the Ancient World, Illustrated History of the World Series,
                                                        Simon and Schuster, 1991
                           The Romans, Living History Series, Wayland
                           A Roman Gladiator, How They Lived Series, Wayland
                           Roman Britain, History in Evidence Series, Wayland

ORDNANCE SURVEY

The Ordnance Survey Map of Roman Britain (1991) is most useful for teachers. It includes a comprehensive index of sites, photographs and a chronological table. From the map it is possible to find the nearest sites to your school, a great help when planning school visits.

THE ERMINE STREET GUARD

This is is an amateur group committed to recreating accurately the appearance and drill of the Roman imperial army of the late first century AD.
For information contact Chris Haines, 'Centurion', The Ermine Street Guard , Oakland Farm, Dog Lane, Witcombe, Gloucester GL3 4UG Tel. 01452 862235

or The Roman Legionary Museum, Caerleon Tel. 01633 423134
English Heritage Special Events Unit Tel. 0171 9733396

PUPILS' RESOURCES - WORKSHEETS

THE GROWTH OF
THE ROMAN EMPIRE

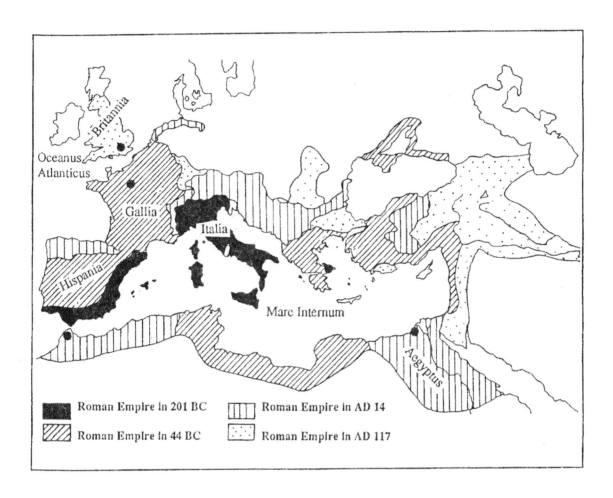

This map shows how the Roman Empire grew.

1. Fill in the modern names under the Latin names on the map.

2. Find out where the following Roman cities are and write them against the dots on the map in Latin and English.

   (a) Alexandria

   (b) Antiochia (Antioch)

   (c) Athenae (Athens)

   (d) Byzantium

   (e) Cartago (Carthage)

   (f) Colonia Agrippina (Cologne)

   (g) Corinthus (Cornith)

   (h) Gades (Cadiz)

   (i) Londinium (London)

   (j) Lugdumum (Lyons)

   (k) Lutetia Parisiorum (Paris)

   (l) Tangio (Tangier))

   (m) Vidobona (Vienna)

A ROMAN WARSHIP

A ROMAN WARSHIP

Look at this drawing of a Roman warship and answer these questions.

1. What was this type of warship called?

2. How was the warship propelled (powered)?

3. Name the structures A, B and C on the warship.

4. Explain how B was used in battle.

5. How fast (or slow) were Roman warships?

6. Why were warships needed by the Romans to invade Britain?

THE ROMAN ARMY

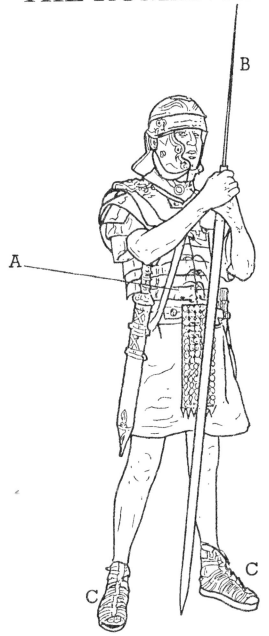

A ROMAN SOLDIER

1. Is this Roman soldier a legionary, a centurion, a standard bearer or auxiliary? How do you know?

2. What was the armour marked A in the picture called?

3. What was B and what how was it used?

4. This type of soldier had three personal weapons. Name them.

5. Which personal weapon usually carried by this soldier is missing from the picture? How was it used?

6. What were the items marked C called? What were they made of and why were they unusual?

HISTORICAL SOURCES

1. *The ordinary soldier carries a javelin and a tall oblong shield. He also carries a saw, a basket, a mattock, an axe, a sickle, a chain and rations to last him three days. He is not very different from a pack mule . . .*

Josephus

What does this passage tell you about a Roman soldier?
Did he have to be weak or strong? Give reasons for your answer.

2. *A legion has builders, carpenters, masons, blacksmiths, painters and all the craftsmen needed to build their winter quarters, to make equipment, towers, fences and siege weapons, and to build and repair weapons, waggons and artillery. There are workshops for shields, breast-plates and bows and where they also make arrows, missiles, helmets and other types of armour. Whatever the army needs is always available in camp.*

Vegetius, *On Military Affairs*

Why do you think all the 'experts' were needed? What does the passage tell you about the way in which the Roman army was organised?

3. *Agricola's object was to accustom the people to a life of peace and quiet by the provision of amenities. He gave private encouragement and official assistance to the building of temples, public squares and good houses ... He educated the sons of the chiefs in the liberal arts ... The result was that instead of loathing the Latin language they became eager to speak it effectively. In the same way, our national dress came into favour and the toga was everywhere ... '*

Tacitus

Give an account of the benefits that Roman rule brought to Britain according to the writer. Were there any disadvantages?

A ROMAN CAMP

1. This drawing shows Roman soldiers setting up camp. Colour the picture and explain what they are doing.

2. Draw a plan of a camp. Show the barracks, the headquarters, where food was stored, the workshops, the rampart, the ditch and gates.

3. Why did the soldiers dig a ditch and build a palisade?

4. All Roman camps were laid out in the same way. What were the advantages of this? Were there any disadvantages?

REASONS FOR INVADING BRITAIN

Read these passages.

A *Remember you are a Roman. It will be your job to rule over other countries, so that the world becomes peaceful and everyone obeys the law.*

Virgil, *The Aneid* 29 - 19 BC

B *Corn, cattle, gold, silver and iron ... these are brought from Britain; also hides, slaves and clever hunting dogs.*

Strabo, *Geography* 1st. century BC

C *The movement had come for which Claudius himself must have longed for, when he could add a new province to the Empire, leading his army in triumph to the native capital and gaining thereby a success worthy of his long line of distinguished ancestors.*

A modern historian, Dr I A Richmond in *Roman Britain* p 22

These are some of the reasons given for the Romans invading Britain.

1. Which do you think is the most convincing reason?

2. Suggest other reasons for the Roman invasions.

**3. What did the Romans (a) gain from the invasion and (b) what did they lose?
Write a short account of any resistance to Rome that you know about?**

4. What do you know about (a) Caractacus and (b) Boudicca?

ROMAN TOWNS AND ROADS

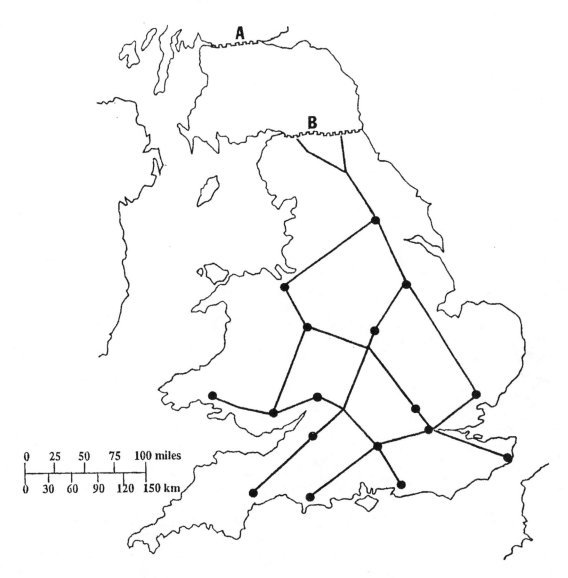

This map shows some of the main Roman towns and roads in Britain.

1. On the map, name the Roman Walls marked A and B.

2. On the map, mark the North Sea and the Irish Sea.

3. On the map, mark Ermine Street, Watling Street and Fosse Way.

4. Write the names of the towns marked with dots on the map.
   Name one town that existed before the Romans came to Britain.

5. Name a town that was already a health resort.

6. Name a town that was already a military site.

7. Describe a Roman town. How were they organised and planned?

8. Compare a typical Roman town with the town in which you live or is nearest
   to you.

A ROMAN VILLA

Look at this drawing and answer these questions.

1. What type of dwelling is this? Is it a large or a small one?

2. Where would it have been found in Roman Britain - town or countryside, north or south? What did it develop from?

3. How many such buildings are thought to have existed?

4. Who lived in such buildings - Romans or Britons?

5. Where were (a) the bedrooms, (b) dining room,(c) kitchen,(d) courtyard, (e) verandah, (f) larders and stores, (g) courtyard and (h) bathouse? Write your answers on the drawing.

6. How were such dwellings kept warm?

7. What decorations existed inside such dwellings? Were there any carpets?

8. What do you understand by a mosaic pavement?

HOW THE ROMANS DINED

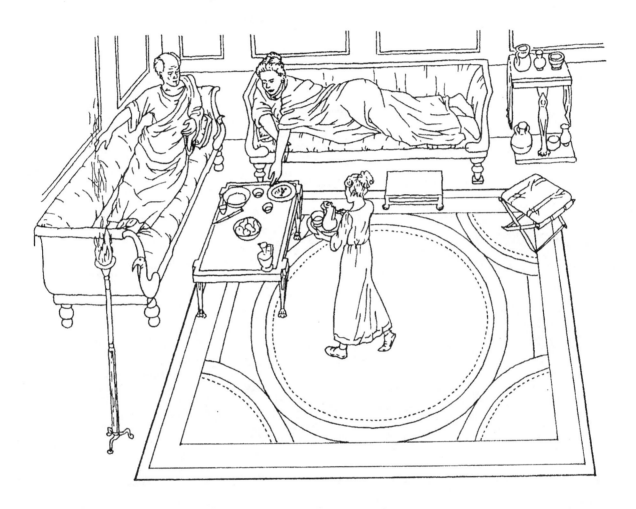

1. There are three people in this picture. Who do you think they are?

2. Imagine you are a guest staying at a Roman villa.
   Write a letter home describing your visit. Include an account of a meal you
   had.

3. Your are a slave in a Roman villa owned by a wealthy Roman citizen.
   Your duties are to help look after the family at meal times.
   Give an account of your work.

ROMAN MEALS

Some Roman delicacies: eggs, shellfish, snails fattened on milk, stuffed dormice, doves, roast boar, honey cakes, spiced loaf, stuffed dates.

1. Colour this drawing.

2. What do you think is being prepared?

3. If you lived in Roman times what would you usually have for breakfast?

4. Explain what is meant by the 'prandium'. Suggest what would have been eaten then.

5. What was the main Roman meal?
   Imagine you are a Roman and write a letter to a friend giving an account of a meal you have enjoyed.

MAKE A MOSAIC

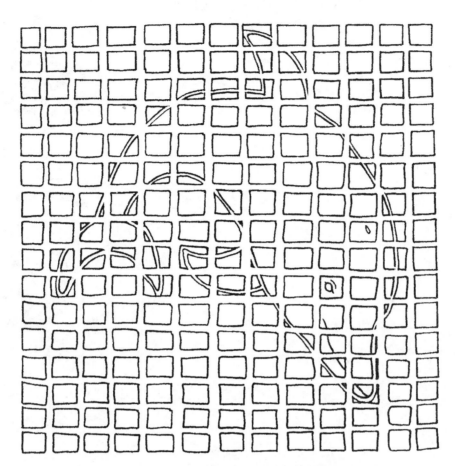

Colour this mosaic to show the pattern made by the different tiles.

To make yor own mosaic, you need the following materials: a large sheet of white paper, a pencil, scissors, paste or glue and pieces of coloured paper.

Cut the coloured paper into tiny pieces to represent tiles.

Cover the backs of the coloured pieces of paper with glue and stick on to the white paper leaving a small space between them to look like plaster. (It is easier to use sticky back paper.)

A ROMAN RECIPE

The Romans like to eat stuffed dates for dessert. You need

> 1 chopped apple
> A handful of nuts
> Crumbs from a small cake
> Pinch of cinnamon or nutmeg
> Half a cup of orange juice

First remove the stones and cut off the hard tops of the dates. Place all the other ingredients in a bowl and mix together with a fork. Place these ingredients into the dates and serve. (Today, this is delicious with ice cream on top.)

ROMANO - BRITISH TIMELINE

These dates and events are muddled. Match each event with its correct date.

Write them out in chronological order beginning with 55 BC.

43 AD	First Roman invasion of Britain by Julius Caesar.
55 BC	Emperor Claudius invaded Britain.
43 - 54 AD	Revolt of Boudicca.
54 BC	King Prasutagus of the Iceni died.
59 AD	Second Roman invasion of Britain by Julius Caesar.
59 - 60 AD	Roman conquest of Britain.
117 AD	Hadrian's Wall began.
122 AD	Emperor Trajan died.
128 AD	Hadrian's Wall completed.
69 - 79 AD	Agricola governor in Britain.
79 - 81 AD	Romans advanced to Wales and the north.
286 AD	Britain declared itself independent from Rome.

ROMANO-BRITISH TIMELINE

A ROMAN DICTIONARY QUIZ

Write the answers in the boxes.

MEANING	WORD
1. A large vessel for storing wine.	1
2. A circular building in which gladiators fought.	2
3. The middle part of a Roman private house (domus).	3
4. A public building used for law courts or offices.	4
5. A good luck charm given to children to ward off evil spirits.	5
6. A miniature carving set in a semi-precious stone.	6
7. Soldiers who fight on horseback.	7
8. Soldiers who march and do not ride.	8
9. A unit of 100 men in the Roman army.	9
10. A unit of 8 men in the Roman army.	10
11. A private house occupied by a single family.	11
12. The supreme ruler of all Roman territories at home and overseas.	12
13. Open space in the centre of a Roman town used for markets and trade and the centre of social and political life.	13
14. Famous Emperor who built a wall to stop rebels invading Southern Britain.	14
15. Roman gold coin worth 25 denarii.	15
16. Four of these make one denarius.	16
17. Prisoners and criminals who fought in an amphitheatre.	17
18. Roman primary school.	18
19. Roman writing instrument.	19
20. Writing material the Romans used instead of paper.	20

A ROMAN QUIZ

1. When did Caesar first invade Britain?

2. Give the date of the real conquest of Brtain by the Emperor Claudius.

3. When did Julius Agricola become governor of Britain?

4. What do you understand by a legion?

5. What was a trireme?

6. What was papyrus?

7. Who or what was a province?

8. Name the official garment of a Roman citizen.

9. What was a villa?

10. Who built most villas in Britain - Romans or Britons?

11. Who or what was a mosaic?

12. What is an aqueduct?

13. Name the form of central heating used to heat Roman buildings.

14. Explain what is meant by caligae.

15. What was a gladius?

16. What was the Roman javelin called?

17. Name the metal helmet worn by Roman soldiers.

18. What do you understand by lorrica segmentata?

19. What was the officer commanding a legion called?

20. Name 5 natural products which Rome obtained from Britain.

21. What metals did Rome obtain from Britain?

22. Give the Roman names for (a) Silchester, (b) Buxton and (c) Bath.

23. Where was Deva and Isca Silurum?

24. Who or what were (a) tabernae, (b) thermopolia and (c) pistrina?

25. Give an approximate figure for the number of villas in Britain.

26. Who or what was 'insulae'?

27. Where did the Romans eat their food?

28. Where did Romans receive their guests?

29. Most large houses had a walled garden. What was it called?

30. Give the Roman name for a household shrine.

ROMAN PASTIMES I

A 1. What was this Roman building and what was it used for?
   2. Why was incense used in this building and why was the sand on the floor red in colour?
   3. What do you understand by 'thumbs up'? Why was it important in Roman times?
   4. Write a short account of a combat in this building beginning:
      'It was the festival of Lupercalia and …

B 1. Colour the drawing.
   2. Give the picture a title.
   3. What is the man in the chair holding in his hands.
   4. What is the person to the right of the picture writing with?
   5. What did Romans write on?
   6. There is a deliberate mistake in the drawing. What is it?
   7. Write a short story beginning:
     My name is Cato and I live in a small town in southern Britain. Everyday, early in the morning I am taken to …

ROMAN PASTIMES II

1. Colour this drawing and give it a title.

2. Give the Latin name for the race taking place.

3. Name the building where such a race took place. What was the building in the centre of the track called?

4. How long was each race? How many chariots and teams usually took part? How were they identified? Who directed the race? How was it started?

5. Write an account of a race in which you took part beginning:
   'My name is Julian and by profession I am a charioteer. I remember my most famous race which began on … '

6. Write a brief account of the story of Ben Hur.

EVERYDAY LIFE
OF A ROMAN SOLDIER

1. **This is a list of tasks you might have to do if you lived in Britain as a Roman soldier. Use it to write an account of a soldier's life.**

1. Join up and take an oath of loyalty.
2. Military drill and exercises.
3. Practise javelin-throwing and fencing.
4. Learn to use a sword.
5. Take part in a 30 km (18 miles) route march.
6. Carry all your weapons and equipment to a new camp.
7. Set up camp.
8. Cook food and eat it.

2. **Complete the following passage about Spartacus by filling in the blank spaces.**

It was traditional that when the Romans c . . . . a country they took prisoners who became s . . . . . Many slaves disliked their living conditions and h . . . . their masters. Even in early Roman times there were r . . . . . . against Roman rule. An early p . . . . was a slave called Spartacus. In 73 BC he ran a . . . from a gladiator s . . . . . near Naples and was j . . . . . by others who formed themselves into a huge slave a . . . They plundered the countryside and terrorised the citizens. The powerful R . . . . decided to crush them. It took over two y . . . . . to do so and 6,000 slaves were crucified on c . . . . . . by the side of the Appian W . . the main r . . . from Rome to Capua.

3. **Identify these objects. What is each used for?**

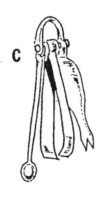

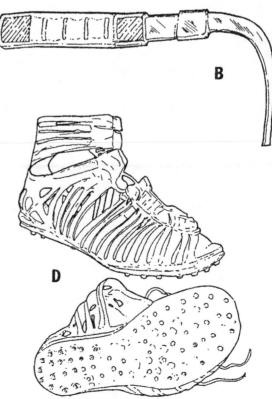

THE ROMAN CHRONICLE

AD 44 Vol. V No. IX
In praise of the Emperor

You are a roving reporter with *The Roman Chronicle* a leading newspaper. Remember to write the heading for all your reports and illustrate them with drawings, paintings or cartoons.

1. You have been asked to go to the local hippodrome to witness an important chariot race. Write an eyewitness account of the race.

[Remember to include the anticipation before the start of the race, the main participants and their exploits so far. Describe the scene, the chariots, the horses, the colours, the atmosphere. The arrival of the Emperor. The start of the race, the noise, smells, fear and excitement, the spills and near misses, how long it lasts. Interview the winner.]

2. Write a letter to your parents or a friend about meeting a famous Roman leader.

3. You have been asked to interview a famous Roman general who has been successful in battle.

[This is an exclusive interview. Include personal details and include a picture (drawing) of the person. Give his name, rank, age, where he was born, grew up and his family. Outline his military career including earlier successes. Give his views on his relationship wiht his men and give your views on his leaderhsip qualities.]

4. The next day you have been sent to see the battle scene and to interview those who have lost.

[Describe the scene - noise, smells, colours, atmosphere. What are the people doing? Burying their dead, recovering their weapons, deciding on revenge. Interview a soldier, a woman and a child. How did they survive and how are they going to cope now?]

5. A year later you return to the battle scene.

[Describe the scene now. Are there any signs of the battle? What has happened to the defeated soldiers. Do the reasons for the battle still exist or have the problems been solved? Are the 'two sides' still enemies or are they able to live in peace with each other? What was the effect of the battle politically and socially?]

ROMAN BATHS AND BATHING

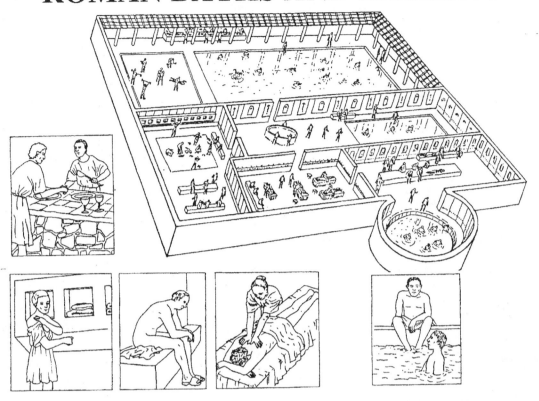

1. Bathing was partly a social activity in Roman times and this picture shows how it was organised. Using this drawing describe the stages in bathing the Roman way. How does the modern leisure centre today compare with a Roman bath?

2. How does the way we bathe today differ from the way Romans bathed? The Romans did not have soap. How did they keep themselves clean?

3. Write three official notices that might have been seen in a Roman baths. The first has been done for you.

> ### DO NOT LEAVE YOUR STRIGILS IN THE GYMNASIUM.

4. Complete the following by filling in the blank spaces.

   Bathing was obviusly very important to the Romans and we can see extensive b . . . . at Buxton in Derbyshire and Bath in S . . . Complete systems of pipes, drains and h . . . . were developed to provide such baths with hot and cold w . . . . The idea of the bath complex was for the b . . . . . . to pass and return to rooms of different t . . . . The usual order was to visit the d . . . . room first, then the cold room followed by the cold plunge bath, then the warm room, the hot room and the hot p . . . . . After s . . . . in the steaming h . . . the skin was scraped with a metal s . . . . . . The bathers then immersed themselves in the hot plunge and then the c . . . plunge to c . . . . their pores.

5. The letters of the following words have been muddled. Find the words which are all to do with Roman baths and bathing.

   (i) SSEGMAA   (ii) BBREARS   (iii) TSILGIR

   (iv) YPCSTUAOH   (v) ACLOCMUNI   (vi) LIO

   (vii) MDAP   (viii) PPSRERGIIN   (ix) TTPMUEERRAE

   (x) DENU.

ROMAN ARITHMETIC

1. A Roman soldier earned 312 denarii a year. Half of his salary was kept for food, equipment and savings. How much did he have to spend each week?
   [1 denarius = 4 sesterii = 16 asses].
   Give your answer (i) in denarii, (ii) in sesterii and (iii) asses.

2. Soldiers were paid in silver denarii or gold coins called aurei.
   If 1 aureus = 25 denarii, how many aurei did the soldier in question 1 earn in a year?

3. Pallus was sent to shop in the market. He bought

   meat costing 3 sesterii 2 asses,
   5 loaves costing 1 ass each,
   fruit costing 1 sesteria,
   wine costing 2 denarii.

   How much change does he have from 4 denarii?
   [Change all the money into asses and give your answer in sesterii and asses.]

4. Julia shops in the market. She buys

   cloth costing 1 denarius,
   shoes costing 6 sesterii,
   a vase costing 3 sesterii.

   If she had 5 denarii at the start of her shopping expedition, how much more money does she need to buy a brooch costing 2 denarii.? Give your answer in asses.

5. Roman numerals

I	II	III	IV	V	VI	VII	VIII	IX	X	XI	XII	XIII	XIV	XV
1	2	3	4	5	6	7	8	9	10	11	12	13	14	15

Roman numerals	L	C	D	M
	50	100	500	1000

What are these numbers?

   XIV   XV   XVI   XXIV   XXXI

Julius is 12 years old. How would he write his age in Roman numerals?

ROMAN RELIGIONS

APHRODITE

_____

ZEUS

_____

HERMES

_____

ATHENA

_____

ARES

_____

APOLLO

_____

These drawings show some of the most important Roman gods.

1. Colour the drawings and write the Roman names under the Greek gods.
   Say all you know about each one.

2. Write a short essay on religious beliefs in Roman times.

3. What other gods in Roman times, personal and public, have you learned about ?

4. Why are the dates AD 313 and AD 394 important as far as religion was concerned?

ROMAN ROADS

1. Colour this drawing of the building of a Roman road.

2. What are the people doing?

3. Name the instrument marked A in the middle of the drawing. What was it used for? What is B?

4. Is the road nearly completed or just started? Give reasons for your answer.

5. Write a short account of 'Road Building in Roman Times'.

6. Compare Roman roads with modern roads under the headings:

   Roman Roads   Modern British Roads

ROMAN MILESTONES

The Romans placed stones along the roads of Britain 1,000 Roman paces apart (48 metres) to show distances. The Latin word 'mille' means 1000. The stone would show the name of the ruling Emperor and the distance to the nearest town or camp. Design a milestone. Give such useful details for travellers, e.g. the name of the road, the number of the road, the distance to the next village, the number of the next town, and the name of the ruler.

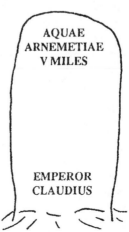

THE ROMANS IN WALES

1. Write the following in the order in which they happened.

(a) Small Roman fort built at Caerwent.
(b) Suetonius Paulinus defeated the Druids.
(c) Ostorius Scapula defeated Caradog.
(d) Roman fort built at Isca Silurum.
(e) Roman villa built at Llantwit Major.

2. The heads and tails of these statements have been mixed. Write them out correctly.

(a) The Druids
(b) The Silures
(c) Caradog
(d) Ostorius Scapula
(e) Suetonius Paulinus
(f) Julius Fontius

(i) subdued the Welsh in South Wales.
(ii) was the Roman Governor who defeated Caradog.
(iii) defeated the Druids in Anglesey.
(iv) were one of the four main Celtic tribes who opposed the Romans.
(v) were the priests of the Celtic tribes.
(vi) was the leader of the rebellion in Wales against the Romans.

3. There were three major forts in Roman Britain: at Chester (Deva), Caerleon on Usk (Isca Silurum) and York (Eburacum). They were all built to the same plan. They were rectangular with a ditch and rampart. There were four gates with a road leading from each gate into the fort. The headquarters (principia) and commanding officer's quarters were in the centre. So were the the stores and workshops. The barracks for the soldiers were set up in rows. Draw a plan of the fort at Isca Silurum. The outline and some of the buildings are drawn for you.

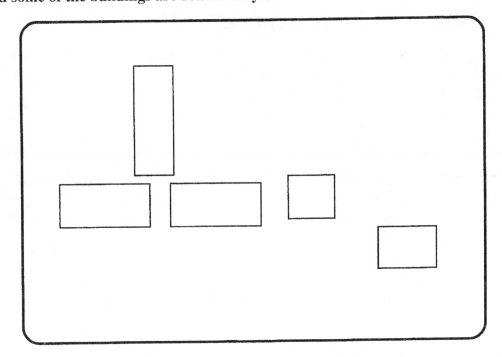

4. Imagine you are a legionary. Give and account of a day in your life at the Isca Silurum fort.

THE LEGACY OF ROME

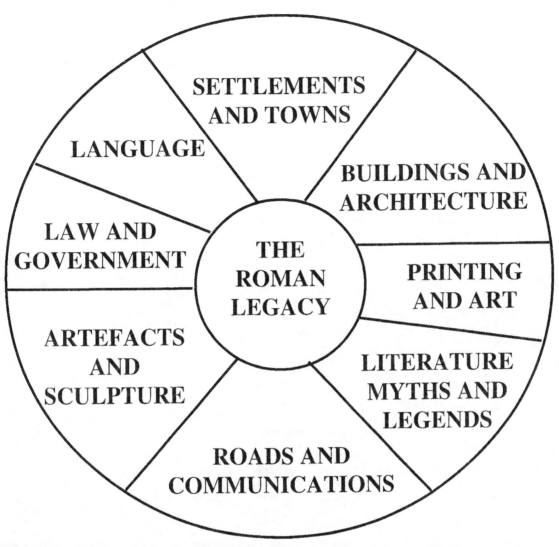

Make this Roman Legacy Wheel the centre of a Roman Legacy Wall.
Your wall could show some of the following.

1. **Settlements and towns** - draw a Roman fort or town. Name present-day places
   and towns in Britain that grew from Roman settlements.

2. **Buildings** - draw a domus and villa.

3. **Language** - make a list of British words that come from Latin.

4. **Art** - the Romans made mosaic pavements. Make a moasic.

5. **The Roman Navy** - drawings and details of warships and commercial vessels.

6. **The Roman Army** - drawings of Roman soldiers and their uniforms.

7. **Roman Religion** - list the gods and their Greek equivalents.

8. **Roman Festivals** - name them and give their importance.

9. **Roman Defence Systems** - fortifications including Hadrian and Antonine Walls.

10. **Roman Life** - including organisation of Roman baths.

PROJECT IDEAS

1. Roman Life.
2. Roman Army Uniforms and Equipment.
3. Roman Dress.
4. Food and Cooking in Roman Times.
5. Farming in Roman Times.
6. Roman Mosaic Pavements.
7. The Art of Defence in Roman Times.
8. Religion and the Romans.
9. Roman Superstitions and Customs.
10. The Roman Legacy.
11. Roman Jewellery.
12. Roman Weapons.
13. Roman Sites Today.
14. Investigation of a Roman Site.
15. A Roman Villa or Roman Villas.
16. Roman Baths.
17. The City of Bath in Roman Times.
18. Roman Society and Class Structure.
19. Women in Roman Society.
20. Jobs and Occupations in Roman Society.
21. Roman Medicine.
22. Roman Roads.
23. Why we should investigate Roman Britain.
24. Hadrian's Wall.
25. The Antonine Wall.
26. British Opposition to Roman Rule.
27. Roman Burials.
28. A Roman Town.
29. Life of a Roman Soldier.
30. Life of a Roman Slave.
31. Roman Recipes.
32. A Visit to a Roman Site.
33. Roman Mathematics.
34. Roman Money.
35. The Rise of the Roman Empire.
36. The Fall of the Roman Empire.
37. Julius Caesar and Britain.
38. The Roman Language.
39. A Roman Biography.
40. Romans - Invaders and Settlers.

THINGS TO MAKE

1. Model of a Roman town.
2. Model of a Roman fort.
3. Model of a Roman villa.
4. A Roman bookmark.
5. A Roman paperweight. (Paint a Roman soldier on a smooth pebble or shell.)
6. A Roman brooch.
7. Roman armour.
8. A Roman toga.
9. An aquilifer.
10. Roman sword.
11. Roman shield.
12. Roman lance.
13. Roman helmet.
14. A desk tidy decorated with Roman pictures.
15. A tidy box decorated with Roman pictures.
16. A mosaic.
17. Puppets of Roman characters for a puppet play.
18. Section of a Roman road.
19. A Roman writing tablet or scroll.
20. Roman sandals.

THE ROMAN GAME

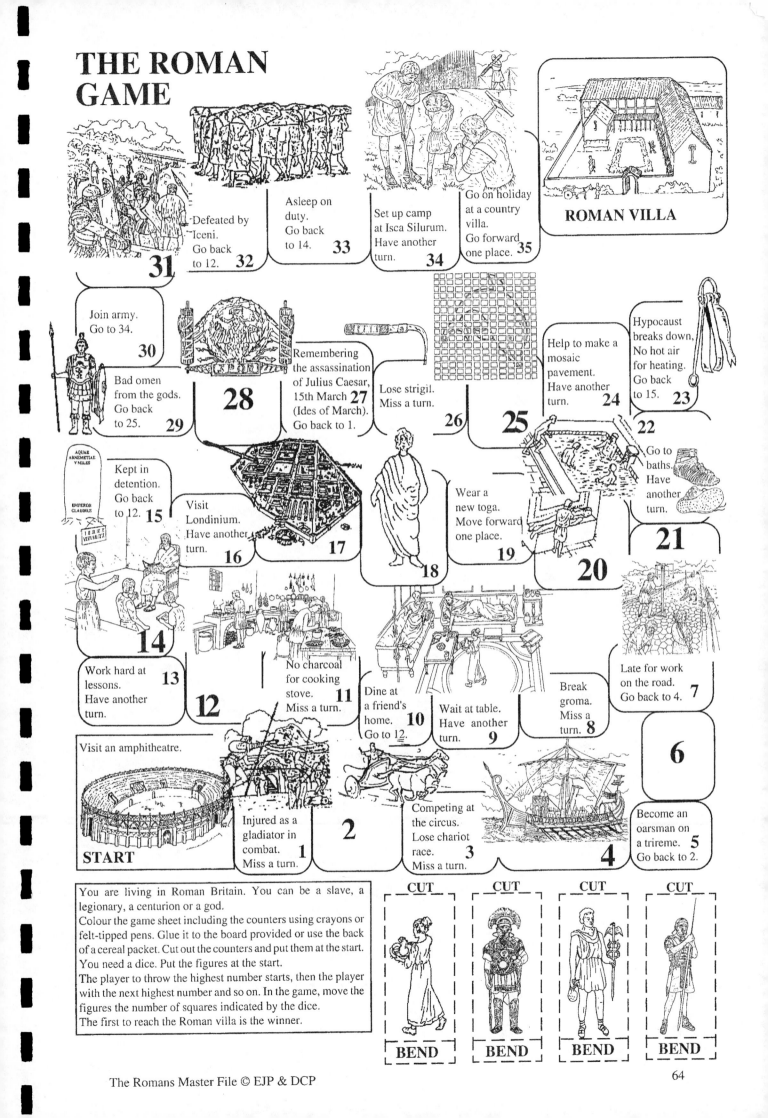

ROMAN VILLA

31 Defeated by Iceni. Go back to 12.

32 Asleep on duty. Go back to 14.

33

34 Set up camp at Isca Silurum. Have another turn.

35 Go on holiday at a country villa. Go forward one place.

30 Join army. Go to 34.

29 Bad omen from the gods. Go back to 25.

28

27 Remembering the assassination of Julius Caesar, 15th March (Ides of March). Go back to 1.

26 Lose strigil. Miss a turn.

25

24 Help to make a mosaic pavement. Have another turn.

23 Hypocaust breaks down, No hot air for heating. Go back to 15.

22

21 Go to baths. Have another turn.

20

19 Wear a new toga. Move forward one place.

18

17

16 Visit Londinium. Have another turn.

15 Kept in detention. Go back to 12.

14

13 Work hard at lessons. Have another turn.

12

11 No charcoal for cooking stove. Miss a turn.

10 Dine at a friend's home. Go to 12.

9 Wait at table. Have another turn.

8 Break groma. Miss a turn.

7 Late for work on the road. Go back to 4.

6

START Visit an amphitheatre.

1 Injured as a gladiator in combat. Miss a turn.

2

3 Competing at the circus. Lose chariot race. Miss a turn.

4

5 Become an oarsman on a trireme. Go back to 2.

You are living in Roman Britain. You can be a slave, a legionary, a centurion or a god.

Colour the game sheet including the counters using crayons or felt-tipped pens. Glue it to the board provided or use the back of a cereal packet. Cut out the counters and put them at the start. You need a dice. Put the figures at the start.

The player to throw the highest number starts, then the player with the next highest number and so on. In the game, move the figures the number of squares indicated by the dice.

The first to reach the Roman villa is the winner.

CUT   CUT   CUT   CUT

BEND   BEND   BEND   BEND

ANSWERS

There may be alternative answers to some questions.

Page 39 Map Growth of Roman Empire

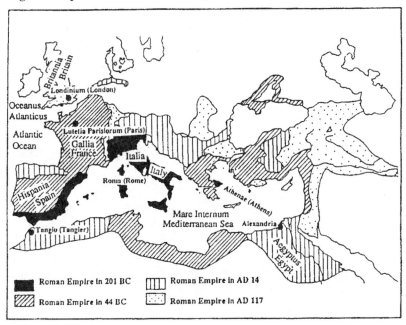

Page 40 Roman Warship

1. Trireme.
2. By sail and by oars.
3. (A) the sail (B) the corvus (C) oars.
4. The corvus had an iron spike which was lowered on to an enemy ship. It held the ship fast as soldiers crossed the drawbridge and engaged in arm-to-arm combat with the enemy.
5. Travelled at about 19km (12 miles) an hour.
6. The only way to reach Britain was to cross the English Channel by ship.

Page 41 Roman Army

1. A legionary. Because of the way he is dressed.
2. Lorica segmentata - overlapping segments of thin iron sheets.
3. A javelin. It was thrown at the enemy.
4. Personal weapons - a javelin (each soldier had two), a sword and dagger.
5. A shield (scutum). This was used to protect the arms and legs. It was used defensively against enemy javelins and arrows and in defensive formations. It was also used to push an enemy off-balance and to parry sword blows.
6. Caligae, open-work boots cut from a single piece of leather. They were laced high up the shin and had thick soles studded with hobnails.

Page 42 Historical Sources See Teachers' Notes.

Page 43 Roman Camp - see Teachers' Notes.

Page 44 Reasons for Invading Britain

1. The raw materials and foodstuffs mentioned by Strabo.

2. Greed, Claudius's ambition, request from Britons to invade. Britons help to Gaul which Rome disliked.
3. (a) Raw materials including supplies of lead (used to extract silver) (b) many soldiers were killed.
4. See Teachers' Notes.

Page 45 Roman Towns and Roads

4. London.   5. Buxton.
6. Colchester.   7. See Teacher' Notes.

Page 46 A Roman Villa

1. A small villa.
2. Countryside, south, a farmhouse.
3. About 500.
4. Britons.
5. See marked plan in Teachers' Notes.
6. By a hypocaust.
7. Paintings on the walls, mosaic pavements on floors. No.
8. A patterned floor consisting of coloured pieces stuck to plaster.

Page 47 How the Romans Dined

1. Master, mistress and slave.

Page 48 Roman Meals

2. A Roman meal.
3. Bread, wheat biscuits, honey, figs, dates or olives. Water or wine to drink.
4. Lunch - bread, left-overs from the meal the night before, figs, dates and walnuts.
5. The cena.

Page 50 Romano-British Timeline

55 BC - 1st. Roman invasion of Britain by Julius Caesar.
54 BC - 2nd Roman invasion of Britain by Julius Casear.
43 AD - Emperor Claudius invaded Britain.
43-54 AD - Roman conquest of Britain.
59 AD - King Prasutagus of the Iceni died.
59 - 60 AD - Revolt of Boudicca.
69 - 79 AD - Romans advanced to Wales and the North.
79 - 81 AD - Agricola Govemor in Britain.
117 AD - Emperor Trajan died.
122 AD - Hadrian's Wall started.
128 AD - Hadrian's Wall completed.
286 AD - Britain declared itself independent from Rome.

Page 51 Roman Dictionary Quiz

1. Amphora (*pl.* amphorae)
2. Amphitheatre
3. Atrium
4. Basilica
5. Bulla
6. Cameo
7. Cavalry
8. Infantry
9. Century
10. Contubernium
11. Domus
12. Emperor
13. Forum
14. Hadrian
15. Aureus
16. Sisterii
17. Gladiators
18. Ludus
19. Stylus
20. Papyrus

Page 52 Roman Quiz

1. 55 BC
2. 43. AD
3. 78. AD
4. A unit of the Roman army of 3,000 to 5,000 men.
5. A warship.
6. Writing material made from a reed.
7. Any area outside Rome that was under Roman control.
8. The toga.
9. A house built in the country usually owned by a wealthy citizen.
10. Britons.
11. Patterns and pictures made up of small coloured pieces of stone and brick set into plaster while it was wet and used to decorate Roman floors.
12. A channel or pipe for carrying water.
13. Hypocaust.
14. Heavy leather shoes studded with hobnails and worn by Roman soldiers.
15. A two-edged Roman sword about 60 cm (2 feet long).
16. A pilum.
17. A galea.
18. Armour wom by Roman soldiers consisting of metal strips.
19. A legate or legatus legionis.
20. Wool, leather, corn, fruits and oil.
21. Silver, gold, tin, iron, lead and copper. Lead because it was available in quantity and was needed to extract silver.
22. (a) Calleva, (b) Aquae Amemetiae and (c) Aquae Sulis.
23. Chester and Caerleon.
24. (a) Inns, (b) snack bars and (c) bakeries.
25. 500.
26. Large apartment blocks or spaces/squares in towns.
27. In a dining room called a triclinium.
28. In the atrium.
29. A peristylium.
30. A lararium.

Page 53 Roman Pastimes I

A

1. An amphitheatre used to stage public entertainment - contests between animals and animals, men and animals and men and men - gladiators.
2. To hide the smells from injured and dead animals and men. To hide the blood.
3. This was understood to be the signal for allowing a wounded gladiator to live. Thumbs down usually meant the death of the gladiator.

B

2. A Roman Schoolroom/Classroom.
3. A scroll.
4. A stylus.
5. On pottery, wax tablets and papyrus.
6. At this time there were no books like the ones on the wall shelf.

Page 54 Roman Pastimes II

1. The Chariot Races.
2. Chariot race - Ludi cirenses.
3. Hippodrome or circus. The spina.
4. Seven laps. 12 chariots and four teams. They wore different colours - red, green, blue and white. The Emperor. He threw a white cloth from a raised platform.

Page 55 Everyday Life of a Roman Soldier

2. It was traditional that when the Romans **conquered** a country they took prisoners who became **slaves.** Many slaves disliked their living conditions and **hated** their masters. Even in early Roman times there were **revolts** against Roman rule. An early **prisoner** was a slave called Spartacus. In 73 BC he ran **away** from a gladiator **school** near Naples and was **joined** by others who formed themselves into a huge slave **army.** They plundered the countryside and terrorised the citizens. The powerful **Roman** army decided to crush them. It took over two **years** to do so and 6,000 slaves were crucified on **crosses** by the side of the Appian **Way** the main **road** from Rome to Capua.

3. (A) Emblem at the top of a legion standard. Each legion had an eagle made of silver called an aquila. It was carried into battle by a soldier, the aquilifer.

(B) A strigil. The Romans did not have soap. They rubbed oil over their bodies and scraped the oil and dirt off with a strigil.

(C) Romans used this in several ways to keep themselves clean.

On the right is a nail cleaner or blackhead remover. In the middle is a tweezers for plucking eyebrows.

On the left is a ear scoop for cleaning inside the ears.

(D) Soldiers' shoes (caligae) made of thick leather. They had hobnails on the soles so that they could carry heavy loads without slipping and not sink in the mud.

Page 57 Roman Baths and Bathing

1. See Teachers' Notes.

4. Bathing was obviously very important to the Romans and we can see extensive **baths** at Buxton in Derbyshire and Bath in **Somerset.** Complete systems of pipes, drains and **hypocausts** were developed to provide such baths with hot and cold **water.** The idea of the bath complex was for the **bathers** to pass and return to rooms of different **temperatures.** The usual order was to visit the **dressing** room first, then the cold room followed by the cold plunge bath, then the warm room, the hot room and the hot **plunge.**

After **sweating** in the steaming **heat** the skin was scraped with a metal **strigil.** The bathers then immersed themselves in the hot plunge and then the **cold** plunge to **close** their pores.

5. (i) Massage **(ii)** barbers **(iii)** strigil
(iv) hypocaust **(v)** laconicum **(vi)** oil **(vii)** damp
(viii) perspiring **(ix)** temperature **(x)** nude

Page 58 Roman Arithmetic

1. (i) 3 denarii **(ii)** 12 sesterii   **(iii)** 48 asses

2. 12 aurei 12 denarii

3. 2 sesterii 1 as

4. 4 asses

5. 14 (XIV),   15(XV),   24 (XXIV),
   31(XXXI)

Julius is XII

Page 59 Roman Religions

1. Aphrodite - Venus;   Zeus - Jupiter;
Hermes - Mercury;   Athena - Minerva;
Ares - Mars; Apollo - Apollo..

See Teachers' Notes.

4. AD 313 - Romans allowed Christianity to be practised. (Emperor Constantine)
AD 394 - Christianity declared to be the official Roman religion.

Page 60 Roman Roads

2. Building a road.

3. (A) A groma used to ensure the roads were straight and direct.
   (B) A ditch for drainage.

4. Nearly completed. The blocks being added in the drawing formed the surface of the road.
(Diagram showing the structure of Roman roads is in the Teachers' Notes.)

Page 61 Romans in Wales

1. (c) AD 51   **(b)** AD 60
   (d) AD 74 or 75   **(a)** AD 75 - 80
   (e) AD 150

2. (a) and **(v)**   **(b)** and **(iv)**
   (c) and **(vi)**   **(d)** and **(ii)**
   (e) and **(iii)**   **(f)** and **(i)**

RECORD SHEET
INVADERS AND SETTLERS
THE ROMANS

Name _____ Age_____

Page Copy Master		Page Copy Master	
39 The Growth of the Roman Empire		53 Roman Pastimes I	
40 A Roman Warship		54 Roman Pastimes II	
41 The Roman Army		55 Everyday Life of a Roman Soldier	
42 Historical Sources		56 *The Roman Chronicle*	
43 A Roman Camp		57 Roman Baths and Bathing	
44 Reasons for Invading Britain		58 Roman Arithmetic	
45 Roman Towns and Roads		59 Roman Religions	
46 A Roman Villa		60 Roman Roads	
47 How the Romans Dined		60 Roman Milestones	
48 Roman Meals		61 The Romans in Wales	
49 Make a Mosaic		62 The Legacy of Rome	
49 A Roman Recipe		63 Project Ideas	
50 Romano-British Timeline		63 Things To Make	
51 A Roman Dictionary Quiz		64 Roman Game	
52 A Roman Quiz			

DOMINO

FIRST STEPS
MASTER FILES
LEARN ENGLISH

Educational resource books at their best. Essential for teachers, home tutors and their pupils. Written by experienced teachers with lesson plans, teaching strategies and notes in each book. Photocopiable with full answers.

Domino Books
(Wales) Ltd
PO Box 32, Swansea
SA1 1FN

Direct from us by post or
Phone 01792 459378
Fax 01792 466337
sales@dominobooks.co.uk
www.dominobooks.co.uk

NATIONAL CURRICULUM

MASTER FILES
FIRST STEPS
TEFL

MASTER FILES
FIRST STEPS
LEARN ENGLISH (TEFL)

Published by
Domino Books (Wales) Ltd
ESTABLISHED SERIES
prepared by experienced teachers

- NOTES FOR TEACHERS AND WORKSHEETS FOR PUPILS IN ONE BOOK
- COMPREHENSIVE COVERAGE
- THERE IS NO NEED TO BUY ADDITIONAL MATERIAL
- ALL THE MATERIAL IS PHOTOCOPIABLE
- EXCELLENT VALUE
- SAVES YOU TIME AND MONEY
- VISUALLY STIMULATING
- BOOKS SPECIFICALLY DESIGNED
- FULL OF TEACHING STRATEGIES AND IDEAS
- READY-TO-USE LESSONS
- FLEXIBLE RESOURCES
- CAN BE USED BY THE WHOLE CLASS, BY GROUPS OR BY INDIVIDUAL PUPILS
- TRIED AND TESTED MATERIALS
- PHOTOCOPIABLE SHEETS TO USE AS THEY ARE OR TO REDUCE OR ENLARGE

AVAILABLE FROM
ALL BOOKSELLERS

Domino Books (Wales) Ltd.
P O Box 32, Swansea SA1 1FN
Tel. 01792 459378   Fax. 01792 466337
www.dominobooks.co.uk
email   sales@dominobooks.co.uk

ORDER FORM OVERLEAF

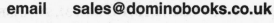

MASTER FILES   FIRST STEPS   TEFL ORDER FORM

KEY STAGE 1 (Age 5 - 7)   **KEY STAGE 2 (Age 7 - 11)**   **KEY STAGE 3 (Age 11 - 14)**

Quantity	Title	ISBN	Price	Cost
	KS1 ENGLISH	1 85772 111 X	£20.00	£
	KS1 MATHEMATICS	1 85772 107 1	£20.00	£
	KS1 MENTAL MATHEMATICS	1 85772 154 3	£20.00	£
	KS1 SCIENCE	1 85772 108 X	£20.00	£
	KS1 DEVELOPING ICT SKILLS	1 85772 166 7	£20.00	£
	KS1 HISTORY	1 85772 112 8	£20.00	£
	KS2 ENGLISH	1 85772 085 7	£20.00	£
	KS2 MATHEMATICS	1 85772 086 5	£20.00	£
	KS2 SCIENCE	1 85772 087 3	£20.00	£
	KS2 DEVELOPING ICT SKILLS	1 85772 165 9	£20.00	£
	KS2 ICT DATA AND SPREADSHEETS	1 85772 167 5	£20.00	£
	KS3 ENGLISH	1 85772 127 6	£20.00	£
	KS3 MATHEMATICS	1 85772 126 8	£20.00	£
	KS3 SCIENCE	1 85772 128 4	£20.00	£
	KS3 ICT DATA AND SPREADSHEETS	1 85772 164 0	£20.00	£
HISTORY				
	KS2 Invaders and Settlers, The Celts	1 85772 067 9	£15.95	£
	KS2 Invaders and Settlers, The Romans	1 85772 070 9	£15.95	£
	KS2 Invaders and Settlers, The Vikings	1 85772 069 5	£15.95	£
	KS2 Life in Tudor Times	1 85772 076 8	£15.95	£
	KS2/KS3 Victorian Britain	1 85772 077 6	£15.95	£
	KS2 - KS3 Second World War	1 85772 121 7	£20.00	£
	KS2 Britain since 1930 (Sept 05)	1 85772 078 4	£20.00	£
	KS2/KS3 Castles	1 85772 075 X	£15.95	£
	CHRISTMAS (AGES 5 - 12)	1 85772 065 2	£20.00	£
TEFL	Learn English	1 85772 174 8	£15.95	£
	Phonics and Spelling (Jan 06)	1 85772 282 5	£15.95	£
EARLY YEARS				
	First Steps Basic Activities in the 3Rs	1 85772 130 6	£12.50	£
	First Steps Number and Counting	1 85772 133 0	£12.50	£
	First Steps Beginning to Read	1 85772 138 1	£12.50	£
	First Steps Beginning to Write	1 85772 139 X	£12.50	£
	First Steps Beginning Mental Maths	1 85772 142 X	£12.50	£
	First Steps Mental Maths, 5 - 6 years	1 85772 143 8	£12.50	£
	First Steps Mental Maths, 6 - 7 years	1 85772 146 2	£12.50	£
	First Steps Mental Maths, 7 - 8 years	1 85772 147 0	£12.50	£
	First Steps Mental Maths 8 - 9 years	1 85772 148 9	£12.50	£
	First Steps Developing Literacy Skills 4 - 5 years	1 85772 151 9	£12.50	£
	First Steps Developing Literacy Skills 5 - 6 years	1 85772 152 7	£12.50	£
	First Steps Developing Literacy Skills 6 - 7 years	1 85772 153 5	£12.50	£
	First Steps Developing Literacy Skills 7 - 8 years	1 85772 177 2	£12.50	£
	First Steps Developing Literacy Skills 8 - 9 years (Nov 05)	1 85772 178 0	£12.50	£
	First Steps Phonics and Spelling 7 - 12 years (Jan 06)	185772 2892	£12.50	£
	Reading and Comprehension 5 - 7 years, Book 1	1 85772 144 6	£12.50	£
	Reading and Comprehension 5 - 7 years, Book 2	1 85772 145 4	£12.50	£

Name/Organisation/School

Address

Post Code   **Tel.**

Contact   **Signature**

Order Number

Date

AVAILABLE FROM ALL BOOKSELLERS OR DIRECT FROM

DOMINO BOOKS (WALES) LTD, P O BOX 32, SWANSEA SA1 1 FN.

Tel. 01792 459378   Fax. 01792 466337

www.dominobooks.co.uk   email: sales@dominobooks.co.uk

TOURIST BOOKS, ACTIVITY PACKS: Please send for lists or see our web site.